PRIMAL

PRAISE FOR *PRIMAL*

"Are you stressed out? Do you want to foster healthier relationships? This well-written, engaging book will help you reconnect to your primal self, leading to a happier, healthier you." —Nicole Apelian, Ph.D., co-star of the television show *Alone*, seasons 1 and 2

"Through stories that invoke passion and practical pathways toward connection, *Primal* asks us to explore what it means to be human . . . this book is not just for people wanting to walk away from modern comforts, but to embrace the wild instincts in all of us." —Doniga Markegard, author of *Dawn Again: Tracking the Wisdom of the Wild*

"*Primal* is a fascinating look at why getting a heavy dose of nature is more critical than it ever has been in human history. Nate Summers asks the deeper question of why paleo diets, crossfit, and survival shows are so popular—and how that relates to the animal that lives within all of us." —Dan Corcoran, survival skills instructor/program director of the Wilderness Awareness School and author of *Ignite*

"What is it about making fire that is so magical? What about the mystery of long-lost primitive survival skills and the simple curiosity about what our pre-agricultural ancestors ate? In this book, you meet people who asked the same questions, then dedicated their lives to seeking the answers. Like you, they were searching for something lost long ago—a window to who we really are and a way to make sense of the world we have inherited." —Tamarack Song, founder of the Teaching Drum Outdoor School and author of *Becoming Nature*

PRIMAL

Why We Long to Be Wild and Free

NATE SUMMERS

Guilford, Connecticut

Dedicated to John "Five Bears" White,
founder of the Ancient Lifeways Institute,
storyteller, teacher, and mentor extraordinaire.
Rest in Peace.

FALCON®

An imprint of The Rowman & Littlefield Publishing Group, Inc.
4501 Forbes Blvd., Ste. 200
Lanham, MD 20706
www.rowman.com

Falcon and FalconGuides are registered trademarks and Make Adventure Your Story
is a trademark of The Rowman & Littlefield Publishing Group, Inc.

Distributed by NATIONAL BOOK NETWORK

British Library Cataloguing in Publication Information available

Library of Congress Cataloging-in-Publication Data available

ISBN 978-1-4930-4463-4 (paper)
ISBN 978-1-4930-4464-1 (e-book)

♾™ The paper used in this publication meets the minimum requirements of American
National Standard for Information Sciences—Permanence of Paper for Printed Library
Materials, ANSI/NISO Z39.48-1992.

The author and The Rowman & Littlefield Publishing Group, Inc. assume no liability
for accidents happening to, or injuries sustained by, readers who engage in the activities
described in this book.

Contents

FOREWORD

A RECENT STUDY OUT OF THE UNITED NATIONS REPORTS THAT
one million species today are on the verge of extinction, and this
has alarming implications for human survival. We currently live in
challenging times. There needs to be a rapid awakening of humanity into deeper understanding of our interdependence with all life.
How will this happen? I've started to see a microcosm of transformation occurring in the world through the sharing of ancestral
arts and ways of being. Everything from how we source our food
to how we run and exercise and even how we adopt mindfulness
practices are part of this change. All come from ancient roots. All
are from an ancient set of instructions deeply embedded in our
nervous system. And all are explored in this book.

Primal is a story about all of us, about the human soul looking
for a way to get back home to the ancient and original. Through
the experiences and insights of inspiring people on the front lines
of an emerging trend, we, as a species, find a way home again.
Nate Summers has lived a life that resonates wonderfully with
the themes of *Primal*—a gathering of stories revealing a larger
story. This is an important book—a snapshot of collective longing
among the human family occupying earth right now.

This longing is evident everywhere I go around this world
teaching and consulting about the connection to nature, to ourselves, and to other people with a quality that satisfies our deepest
needs as humans. Indeed, my vision and life's work focuses on
achieving just this—making everyone healthy and happy when

·

rooted in their ancient nervous system. They are not rehabilitated, but habilitated, like in the work of Kathleen Lockyer, an occupational therapist (rxoutside.com) who uses deep nature connection work to treat Nature Deficit Disorder, an epidemic burdening the mental, emotional, physical, and spiritual health of modern people.

Recently I visited my indigenous Naro Bushmen friends in Botswana and spoke to them about our global efforts to connect people to nature, to one another, and to themselves.

"How do you work with your children to connect them so deeply to nature? How did you learn to do that?" we asked the Bushmen. "How do you support each other in living?"

"Well, this is just what we've always done. This is, this is what it means to be a Bushman," the elders replied. I would argue this is what it means to be human, too.

But modern people often don't do these things anymore. As documented in his book, *Last Child in the Woods*, Richard Louv, who coined the term Nature Deficit Disorder, links the loss of a nature connection to rising childhood obesity and other ailments. There's a great need and longing for connection, as many modern people will confirm. And it's not just connection with each other as human beings, but also with one's self and the natural world. As people remember what it means to be a connected human being, profound, global cultural change is possible. *Primal* is part of a wave of many books reflecting this emerging trend.

But *Primal* isn't simply for a core group of primitive life-seeking enthusiasts. Even those who don't actively seek out the "primal" path have deep internal longings too. My cousin, Jeff, and his wife, Kim, for example, do not identify as people focused on primitive skills or nature connection. As recent empty nesters, their lives and perspectives shifted profoundly after a sailing journey and from their experiences gained while disconnecting from their modern lives and going on a deep nature connection. Kim Brown Seely writes about this journey, and of disconnecting to reconnect, in her book, *Uncharted*. Beautiful and healing, these many stories give me hope.

Primal is a thrilling adventure of many experiences and practices that will inspire and create deep curiosity about our collective future on this planet. Perhaps by uncovering these deep longings and understanding them we will find a way forward. This book is really for anyone seeking to discover what it means to be human.

Jon Young
Founder 8 Shields Institute
Author of *What the Robin Knows* and
Coyote's Guide to Connecting with Nature

INTRODUCTION

THE STUDENTS LOOKED LIKE HELL. I'D SEEN GROUP AFTER GROUP of students return from a week of full-on survival immersion before, and while they rarely looked good, I'd never seen them look quite this bad.

"Oh my . . . they look like they've been in a war," Pam quipped quietly to me. Pam was an elder at Wilderness Awareness School (WAS), the Washington State–based school I'd taught at for more than a decade, and she, too, had seen her fair share of students returning from survival trips. The students had been gone for 5½ days, leaving with only the clothes on their backs. After 9 months of training in a variety of wilderness skills, including tracking, survival, leadership, edible and medicinal plants, bird language, natural movement, and community building, the students were in the middle of "The Gauntlet"—the 3-week culmination of testing their skills, themselves, and the bonds that had been forged over the course of the year.

And, honestly, it looked like they had gotten their butts kicked.

Two blonde women, one in her late 20s and the other in her early 30s, emerged first from the bushes. Moss wove through their hair, dirt smudged on their faces, black gunk crusted their hands and nails—all not exactly unusual for a survival immersion—but what struck me most was their eyes. There were dark circles under them and they looked haunted . . . stricken. And these two were two of the leaders of their group. Naturally charismatic, intelligent, poised, and confident, they had been some of the best examples of solid female leadership I had seen at the school in some time, and they looked beaten . . . but not completely broken.

A student's return from a survival trip is often a mixed experience. Of course, there is a lot of hardship, but there is usually triumph and wonder and adventure. I didn't see that in the eyes of the twenty-plus students as they slowly trudged up and gathered around the community fire. As the fire crackled and the smell of seasoned Douglas fir and alder settled around us, what I did see was relief, and even the beginning of tears as warm soup and broth was passed around. There were moans and sighs as elders came and brought warm wool blankets. We sat under the protection of a plastic blue tarp hung above in the trees to keep out the cold rain and mist seeking to seep into our clothes and bodies from all directions. Slowly, through the coaxing of myself and other instructors and facilitators, the wild stories of survival emerged.

Why would students opt to spend days on end battling the natural elements without a single modern comfort between them? Why did hordes of students come from all over the world to pursue this undertaking annually? Why would people take a year out of their lives to learn skills that their ancestors needed 10,000 years ago, skills that are mostly irrelevant in a world of Facebook, iPhones, and Amazon?

For me, the answers to these questions lay in the past, in my own teenage years where I, too, was immersed in a Stone Age world for weeks at a time. The answers were in a place and space where I found what it was like to live like ancient people did—even for a short period of time. Those summers in the hardwood forest of southern Illinois, running free and wild through the trees, shaped so much of who I was and who I came to be. I remember the first time I made a fire with a bow-drill friction fire kit, sweat pouring down my face, my arm ready to fall off from fatigue, and the sweet smell of thick smoke as a tiny ember was birthed. And that was just fire.

Wandering riverbeds to collect rocks and shape them into stone tools with bones and basic copper tools; throwing wooden darts from an ancient spear-thrower (atl-atl) at a deer-shaped target again and again and finally hitting it and knocking it over with a look of disbelief; scraping thick fat off a buffalo hide with bone tools while swatting at flies under a glaring sun. These were just some of the unusual experiences that lit me up inside as a teenager. Little did I know what was really happening and what was really awakening.

⁓

Decades later, under a blue plastic tarp, I sat far away from the fire, watching the students gradually thaw and come alive. Surrounded by alumni, elders, instructors, and other community, the pain and weariness of their survival experience waned with the taste of fresh food; being welcomed by song; and—most importantly—being witnessed, heard, and understood as they shared their stories.

Their week hadn't been easy—but survival training never is, and anyone who tells you or sells you otherwise is full of it. Survival training is hard, and even when you gain a mastery over a particular skill, often what arises is humbleness, not arrogance. But the struggle and the hardship are matched with triumph and success, and all of the students had made it back alive. Sure, they had been cold, wet, damp, and miserable at times. They were the only group that I remembered that had to resort to their emergency kit to get their fire going because it rained so hard and fast the first 24 hours they were out. But they survived. And in surviving they triumphed. They had faced a reality that very few people ever face, and they had lived. And now something that had begun to stir throughout their year of training was fully awake and alive.

Teaching survival, wilderness living, and the related skills for over 2 decades has shown me time and time again what happens when people are exposed to ancient ways of living. It has been quite strange and also quite wonderful to watch what was once a relatively obscure field now explode into an international phenomenon. When I was a teenager spending time at the Ancient Lifeways Institute (ALI) in southern Illinois in the early 80s, there were very few schools doing similar things. Now there are schools in almost every state in the United States, and a large number of schools in Europe and Canada, as well. Similar schools are starting in Australia and India. In watching this explosion of schools form, I began to ask myself what was really going on. Why would people shell out hard-earned cash on expensive survival skills classes, when the basic skills you need could be learned in a simple weekend?

After instructing immersion programs for teens and adults on and off for many years, I discovered the answer. I realized that what was happening to people when they dove into these programs was the same thing that happened to me when I was a teenager. That experience kept me going back to the Ancient Lifeways Institute—the world's first Stone Age immersion camp—summer after summer, learning Stone Age living skills from the school's founder and an amazing teacher, mentor, and crazy character named John Five Bears White.

John was a wonderful and strange person pulled from another time. While he didn't fit most people's stereotypical image of a Native American (he didn't have long dark hair, prominent cheekbones and nose, and brownish skin), John did look like he could be from the Stone Age. John and his family were descended from Cherokee, Shawnee, and Scots heritage, and John had an academic background in anthropology serving as adjunct faculty to universities. He was big-boned with ruddy-brown skin, a balding head with wispy gray hair pulled back in a ponytail, and a booming voice. He would wax eloquently about different topics, and then other times grunt gutturally and use his favorite non-word, "Wahhhh!" In a description of John written by his son,

Jonah, John is described as having the thickest bones and one of the densest bodies ever seen. One time, John fell off the roof twice over the course of an hour, and each time he picked himself up, dusted off, and climbed back on the ladder to get to work.

I spent my summers at ALI as a teen under John's crazy Stone Age tutelage, with plenty of help from his wife, Ela, and his very strong, vital, and wild sons, Watie (pronounced "wa-di" and meaning war paint), Jonah (a transliteration of a Cherokee word meaning bear), and Mark. John and his family were my first "survival skills" instructors and mentors. Going to ALI really was like stepping back in time, and it was there that I first learned to track wild animals, move quietly through the woods, listen to what the birds were telling me, catch fish bare-handed, make pottery with clay I dug from the earth, make stone tools, make fire, and feel the deep connection to others doing the same.

ALI fulfilled a deep longing I didn't even realize I had. ALI was situated far off the beaten path outside of a town called Hardin in southern Illinois. You had to take a ferry across the Illinois River to get to the school, and it was nestled in an interesting intersection of heavily forested hills that had narrowly avoided being flattened by glaciers in the last ice age. Illinois is an extremely flat state, mostly made up of monocrop farmland. So the hardwood forested hills, bubbling creek, and open meadows were an inviting landscape much more diverse than what I was used to. Looking back, it is interesting to see the parallels between the landscape surviving the last ice age and the Stone Age skills we learned there.

To refer to the place as a "camp" or "institute" is being very generous with the description. John ran the camp on his own property with his house being a small, rammed earth cabin. Our "accommodations" were in an open-air longhouse called Kaskaskia Lodge with a central fire pit, where we slept on wooden platforms about a foot off of dirt floors, underneath a ceiling made of cattail mats. I loved it. And what I've found is that, over time, everybody loves living like that if they give it a chance, even if just for a short while.

At night, my fellow students and I would gather with John around a fire in one of the lodges and sit on the dirt floor or wooden platforms and hear stories that had been passed down to John. This was what John called our oral tradition time, and little did I realize how lucky and rare it was for me to get to experience this age-old tradition. John shared stories he had heard from many different Native elders, for some of which he was the only orator. The stories opened a portal into a mysterious world of talking animals, powerful elders, gifted young men and women struggling to help their tribes, and—ultimately—stories of what it means to be human in a hunter-gatherer context.

Many years later at Wilderness Awareness School, I would sit in another dirt-floored hut and get to teach and witness hundreds of people coming to life through their own experience of survival, deep nature awareness, connection, and ancestral skills. The central fire pit and African-Akamba-style hut, called *Malalo ya Chui, the Lair of the Leopard* (or, Malalo, as it was often nicknamed), was the core teaching and key ceremonial area at WAS. The lore around the fire pit was that a fire had never been started there by modern means, only with primitive technologies, and that Ingwe (the grandfather of WAS) had laid down the fire pit when there was no building there. He had decreed it the central fire where children and adults alike would gather to share their stories of time in the wilderness.

Wilderness Awareness School started as a relatively small deep nature connection and survival skills school in New Jersey in 1983. It was co-founded by Jon Young, the first student of Tom Brown Jr., one of the most famous figures in the survival skills world, and Norman Powell, aka Ingwe, a man who had grown up deeply immersed in tribal traditions in Africa. The school moved to Washington State in 1995, and exploded in growth after only a few years. It was soon running summer camps for kids all over the Puget Sound area, and it was at one of these camps that I first joined the school as a volunteer instructor in 1997.

I worked for the school on and off as a youth instructor for a couple of years, and then, in 1999, my colleague, Jason Knight, started the first-ever 9-month survival skills and deep nature connection immersion program in the world. This college-level program for adults was called the Wilderness Awareness Residential Program and was designed to dive deep into the world of survival for multiple days every week from September to May. The first year of the program Jason and I were the two core instructors, with other major teachers, such as Jon Young and Heidi Bohan, joining for specific teaching days. This program had ten students its first year, and only six finished.

I pursued other things after that first year, but a decade later when the program was renamed the Anake Outdoor School, in honor of Ingwe, I returned, first as a core instructor and then as a specialty instructor. I also started a follow-up program, called the Anake Leadership Program, that became an instructor training program for adults who had completed the first year of Anake. This became the main pool for future staff and instructors, as WAS exploded in growth both in youth and adult programs, and similar programs took off throughout the country and world.

It was at WAS and at the Anake Outdoor School program next to the sacred fire pit that Ingwe had laid down, in the open-aired, eight-sided structure of Malalo that I saw the same students who had suffered quite heavily on their survival week return alive, vital, and connected. The students had had a couple of days off. They had rested, eaten, showered, and generally reconnected with modern conveniences for at least a short time. They also had probably gone through the completely surreal experience of walking through a grocery store, with its hordes of food, after eating very little for almost a week.

They had just survived two of the three weeks of The Gauntlet.

The Gauntlet was created as a culminating multiweek experience for students who had spent the previous 9 months studying the core curriculum of the school. While a normal week of the Anake program consisted of 3 days of classes interspersed with immersive and intense survival overnights and, sometimes, week-long exploratory expeditions to other sites, The Gauntlet was designed to go beyond all of these other very powerful experiences and help students test and integrate everything they had learned in a 3-week back-to-back-to-back "test" of sorts.

Week 1—the Scout Camp experience—tests awareness skills, and students work in small groups to travel through an unfamiliar landscape with the goal of learning and discovering where all the other small groups are without being seen and discovered. For many, it is the closest we get to being a wild animal for a few days at a time. Week 2—the survival challenge—places students in the wild for days on end with little else but the clothes on their backs.

The third week of The Gauntlet is pretty mellow compared to weeks 1 and 2, though there are plenty of fun surprises left, as well. Week 3 is meant to prepare students for re-entering society while honoring their accomplishments. The students got used to the regular rhythm of sleeping on the land in their tents, being fed three meals a day, being around a fire at Malalo at night, and starting their goodbyes.

One of the things we did as instructors for this final week was to wrap everyone in a fuller, larger sense of community and connection. Elders were brought in to witness their stories and hear where they were heading to next. During one of numerous closing circles, alumni of the program and staff gathered at Malalo and heard what the students were taking with them after a year going deep into this world. Sharing their stories and looking ahead was one of the main steps toward integrating what they had learned and trying to figure out how they would carry it forward. These storytelling sessions were important; however, the crown jewel of

Introduction

the week was one last unexpected challenge . . . a powerful rite
of passage for everyone in the program and a way of feeling the
power of a multigenerational village happening all at once.

When our primal wild selves are awakened, we feel more alive,
wild, free, *human*. And we want to help others feel the same. But
why, in the 21st century, are survival skills so popular? Why are
there so many survival shows on television? Why do we want to
see people "Naked and Afraid" or "Alone"? Why have survival
skills schools exploded in number? And why is all of this happening at a time when we spend more and more time glued to our
smartphones, digitally liking things on social media, hashtagging
our latest venture, and everybody's screen-time keeps increasing?

On some level, we don't really need these survival and ancient
living skills to be successful in our modern world. But people
are obsessed with survival, and once they get a taste they usually
come back for more. And this can irrevocably change their lives
and who they are.

In my years teaching these skills, I realized we were leading
people into an understanding, an awareness, a level of connection
that was *primordially human*. I'm not the only person to have
had this same insight. It's common for teachers of survival and
ancestral skills to understand that we are basically helping people
remember something very fundamental:

*On a basic biological (and neurological level) we are still hunter-
gatherers who desire a degree of nomadic wandering and lots of time
in nature. We spent at least 200,000 years wandering the earth as
hunter-gatherer nomads. During that time, we practiced survival
and Stone Age living full-time. Our time living in our fully civilized,
highly technological society is the blink of an eye in terms of biology,
evolution, and how our brains work.*

This book is a deep dive into this premise and will explore
several facets of human life to directly answer the *why* of it all.

XVII

Why do we watch survival shows? Why do people do survival immersion programs? Why is there now a whole field of exercise based on shedding our shoes and moving through natural landscapes unencumbered, wild and free? What does it mean for us as modern humans and what does it bode for our future?

We will look at several core topics and hear stories and insights from leading experts in the field. Men, women, young, old, indigenous . . . I've combed the landscape for experts in many different areas to share their knowledge of why we do these things and why they are important in our increasingly technologically dependent world. Why are we so disconnected from the enchanting nourishment of bird songs at dawn? Why are we turning our eyes blindly to massive climatic change? Why do we ignore trees and forests dying in massive numbers? And, more importantly, what can we do about it?

So, join me on a journey through the wild, crazy, potent world of modern survival. Hear stories, anecdotes, and insights from a diverse group of experts, and let yourself explore deep parts of yourself. And don't be surprised if you, too, feel a deep longing from within. Your own ancestral self may begin to stir. Perhaps you, too, will discover a new understanding of what it means to be *human*, what it means to be *primal*, and know deeply your own longing to be wild and free.

CHAPTER 1

Sur-thrival: The Boom of Survival Skills in the 21st Century

Let me tell you about fire. Fire is food, warmth, and protection from bears. Fire is life. Always speak to fire. All things you can know if you speak with fire.

—MARIAN, NATIVE KORYAK WOMAN
QUOTED IN *THE RAVEN'S GIFT*

MY ARM ACHED AND THROBBED BEYOND BELIEF. THE STRENGTH in my biceps and triceps faded while my elbow began to feel numb. Sweat covered my brow and stung my eyes as it dripped down my face. I was so tired, as if I had been running for miles. I wanted to give up so badly. But through the smoke pouring up from my bow-drill kit I kept pumping my arm back and forth, pushing down with my left arm as the spindle twirled side to side. After ten more strokes with my kit, I began to weaken. My arm hurt too much, and my spindle started to wobble, threatening to pop out.

Then something changed.

The smell of the smoke became more pungent—sharper and sweeter—and through the billowing smoke I caught a glimpse of an orange-red simmering glow at the base of my fireboard. The dark dust that had been piling up where the spindle met the board had transformed. It was now smoking, simmering, and pulsing with life. Fire had been born, and I had made my first friction fire.

It was so satisfying to carefully place that coal into a bundle of tinder and gently blow it to life. The smoke comes slowly at first, and then it wafts and wafts and often will choke you. The smoke gets so thick that it can be hard to see the tinder bundle as it gets closer to combusting. But, suddenly, the tinder bundle bursts into flame, and light and warmth spread rapidly.

And, of course, in true John Five Bears White style, as I gently blew and gave life to the tinder bundle nest, a story he told us earlier in the week came to mind: a story of a spider slowly rocking a coal in a nest of her webs, gently blowing and giving it life.

Making fire is pure magic that has captivated people for all of time. Whether it's making their first-ever solo fire, making a "5-minute" fire with matches or lighter, or seeing a friction fire with ancient skills, people can't help but be engrossed by fire. I have seen people completely blown away by witnessing a fire made with a bow-drill or hand-drill. Friction fire—or fire made by rubbing two pieces of wood together—is the ultimate attention-grabber, showstopper, and crowd-pleaser.

Part of the experience is the sensory immersion that happens for everyone. There's the squeaking of the bow-drill spindle moving back and forth rapidly in its socket, and there's the obvious effort of the person making the fire—sweat, grunts, the red face, the first wisps of smoke slowly emerging at the intersection of the pieces of wood. A distinctive smell arises as the smoke becomes more vigorous, and the pungent, sweet aroma announces the arrival of a coal. Finally, there's the illumination of a coal blown to flame reflected in the eyes of the firemaker and the audience . . . total crowd-pleaser.

Fire is as primal, primordial, and ancient as humans get. It is the light that drives away the dark. It is what warmed us for millennia. It protected us from wild beasts and cooked our food to help make us smarter. Fundamentally, it made us human. It distinguishes us from animals, and, without it, we wouldn't be who we are. Even before we were humans, we were using fire. Human ancestors and our primate precursors have been working with fire for as many as *1.7 million years.*

I've made hundreds of fires under all sorts of ridiculous conditions: solo, team, wet, cold, snow, dry, hot, in front of crowds, on the dirt floor of Malalo, on sand bars, in the mountains. There's nothing that screams survival more than the ability to make fire. Tom Hanks illustrates this so fully and realistically in the film *Cast Away*, when his character finally makes a Polynesian-style fire plough friction fire after days of effort. After finally achieving success he screams, "I have made fire!!!" I've seen this same look of triumph wash across the faces of hundreds of survival students, both young and old, after hours and hours of struggle. Making fire is often very hard. It can take some students weeks or even months to get their first friction fire. The depiction in *Cast Away* is quite realistic, not just in Hanks's emotions around the triumph but in the real monotony of the hour after hour of challenge to make it work.

It used to be quite common for people to know how to make a quality fire with a lighter or matches. Now, as our human connection to fire becomes more distant due to modern amenities afforded us, this skill is fading. Indoor central heating has taken away our relationship with wood and fire, and many people don't even know how to construct a proper fire structure or even know what components you need to have a successful fire.

But learning to make fire *without* matches or a lighter is much harder and an incredible skill to possess. It's a very empowering feeling for people to learn how to create friction fire. Many of the people who die in real-life survival scenarios die from exposure—a combination of cold and dehydration. Fire-making is one of the first skills people want to learn at survival schools, and is one of the skills that could truly keep you alive.

When I was 17 and attending the Ancient Lifeways Institute, I created my first coal with a bow-drill set, and it took me over 2 hours to start a fire with a pre-made set (a fire kit I didn't make myself). Using a bow-drill involves rapidly moving a bow back and forth with one arm. The bow from the bow-drill is a curved piece of wood with a piece of rope or cordage tied on the two ends, thus forming a bow-like shape. Intertwined in the cordage is a wooden spindle. One end of this spindle rests on a flat board, called a fireboard or hearth, and the other end rests in a wooden handhold. By rapidly moving the bow back and forth with one arm, and the other on the hand-hold, the spindle creates a tremendous amount of friction on the fireboard. It takes 800 degrees of heat generated from the friction to produce ignition in the form of a glowing orange coal.

In retrospect, I wish I had struggled more with that first coal . . . I didn't practice or try to make fire again with a friction fire kit until years later. I thought I had figured it out, that I knew how to make fire. I've found if people succeed early with friction fire, they assume they've mastered the skill, and they don't put in a lot of dirt-time to continue to practice that skill. They will assume that they can replicate those results when they need it. Fire has kicked my ass more than once. It's made me feel hugely successful and self-confident, and it's also made me feel really embarrassed. I've succeeded spectacularly and have failed spectacularly.

There's something extremely fickle about fire, and many students joke about having to pray to the fire gods. Fire is an incredible mentor and teacher, an ultimate reflection of ourselves: our struggles, our egos, our humbleness, our confidence. It is one of the most basic and most important survival skills, and friction fire is a skill that can transcend time and space. It has the power to transport us to our most ancient ancestral memories.

Which makes it really freaking weird that it's now on television all the time.

I remember when the shift happened. Back in the late 90s and early 2000s, when the survival program and school I was a part of was really starting to grow in popularity, most of the students who showed up (both adults and kids) had never seen friction fire in person or on television. Maybe there was a small chance that they had seen it in a movie, like *Cast Away* (which came out in 2000 by the way), but still the vast majority of students had never seen it, and for them it was mind-blowing.

Today, however, while the thrill of seeing it in person hasn't lost any of its mystique, most everyone has seen friction fire before they come to survival school, and usually it's from television (or YouTube or Facebook or Instagram).

On May 31, 2000, *Survivor*, a reality-based television show, debuted on CBS. Over its first 5 years, the show was consistently in the top ten most watched shows on TV. Soon after *Survivor* appeared, other similarly themed survival shows debuted, such as Bear Grylls's flashy *Man vs. Wild* and the gritty, super-realistic *Survivorman*, featuring the highly skilled Les Stroud. Over the first 2 decades of the 21st century, survival-themed shows have continued to grow, and the explosion of shows on television that have used survival as the drive and draw for their audience have been wildly successful. There has been over a 1,000 percent growth in the number of survival-based shows on television since *Survivor* first debuted (now, at the time of this book's printing, in its thirty-seventh season) and this growth has been mirrored in the growth of both survival skills schools and immersion-based survival programs.

So what gives? Why are survival-themed television shows suddenly becoming big business? How did this happen? Why are people willing to spend tens of thousands of dollars to go deeply into the world of survival skills for a whole year of their life?

Let's dig deeper.

In this chapter, we'll look at this boom in survival skills shows and survival skills schools by talking to experts and leaders in the field. You'll hear from people who've been on TV showing these skills, and also from the folks who've been teaching and leading for years or even decades. Together, we'll uncover how the boom in enrollment at survival schools and the immense popularity of survival skills television shows are related and what it means for the world of survival.

— ⁓

It's probably best to first define the term *survival skills*. While it may seem pretty basic, there's actually a lot of confusion around what is or is not a survival skill and the many related terms and ideas. To clarify things, I turned to my friend, Dan Corcoran, an expert survivalist, woodsman, and hunter. Dan and I have been teaching together for over 15 years. We've tracked wild wolves together in remote parts of Idaho; taught flintknapping and stonework to Anake students in the damp, gray winters of the Pacific Northwest; and have also raised our kids together in the same community. Dan is a stocky, solid midwesterner with a personality and diligence that matches his physical profile: solid.

"For me, there are three main categories [of survival skills]. Modern Wilderness Survival, Bushcraft, and Primitive Survival," Dan said.

Dan sees Modern Wilderness Survival as what most people think of when they hear the word *survival*: how to get out of the woods (or the desert or mountains) if something has gone wrong, like getting injured or lost. While all survival skills training includes fire, water, shelter, food, navigation, and orientation, Modern Wilderness Survival also includes learning how to tend to these things with modern gear, especially with whatever you have on you. Dan developed a hugely popular course for Wilderness Awareness School to address these needs, called Survival Basics, that covers fire, food, shelter, water, awareness, orientation, and navigation, but it also addresses what most people come to conquer: fear.

"I wanted to make something like a Wilderness First Aid course—a 2-day course that hikers, mountain bikers, and even people who are afraid to go in the woods could easily do. It's really surprising what people are afraid of. A lot of people come with fear of animal encounters, like cougars or even spiders, but they leave with a deeper understanding of how important it is to stay dry and warm. Hypothermia is a much bigger, [more] realistic concern."

The second category, Bushcraft, adds another layer to survival skills by teaching the creation of ancestral crafts, like bowls, baskets, and wooden spoons, often with limited use of modern tools. There is a liveliness that happens in people when they learn to make things themselves.

"Survival training helps people feel more empowered, self-confident, connected, and grounded," said Dan. "But people also want to be more self-sufficient, and these skills give them that. Yes, it takes a few hours to make a handmade wooden spoon that you could buy for eight dollars. But the point isn't saving time and money."

The point is to make something yourself with your own hands using simple tools. There is a deep satisfaction in making something that is useful by yourself, even if it isn't that pretty. (Dave Canterbury, a star of the show *Dual Survival* and the founder of Pathfinder Survival School, has recently written a series of excellent books all about Bushcraft. They take some of the concepts here and expand upon them greatly, serving as an excellent source for people looking to go deeper with their survival skills.)

Bushcraft can take people deeper into the world of survival, but it isn't the same as going full-on Primitive Survival, the third category. This is the level of survival skill a lot of people search for. It means using no modern gear and being able to survive simply with the clothes on your back.

For Dan, the distinction is important, but not an easy journey, "Modern survival skills are the most practical and easiest to learn. Primitive survival takes a lot of time and dedication. But some folks really crave it. They don't want to be tethered to our modern financial system and society. They want to know they can thrive or at least survive without having to rely on factories to make their clothes."

Many who seek out survival immersion programs are looking for that last piece: freedom from a society that creates reliance and dependence on a system that not everybody agrees with, a system that, seemingly, causes a whole host of problems. At the Anake Outdoor School, Wilderness Awareness School's 9-month immersion program, Dan is the chief survival specialist, where we've co-taught a variety of survival skills, from bow-making and flintknapping to shelter-building and even brain-tanning hides. In an immersion program, you are able to push people harder and go deeper, and you don't have to worry so much about people's edges. They are there to have their psychological and physical edges pushed and challenged.

So what happens when people immerse themselves in survival training?

They come alive with confidence, poise, vitality, and deep connections. As Dan says, "Embracing these birthrights that we have lost brings people alive. They have a huge value in our life. I haven't met anybody that tried this [training] and it really didn't do anything for them. It's always a lightning bolt."

But why?

For Dan, it's not complicated. "Because we're continuing to get more and more disconnected from nature, and these skills are buried deep within us. They are in our DNA. They are primal. They are part of the human operating system. We're designed for these skills: to eat wild foods, to move our bodies, and to be in wild places."

When I tracked Dan down to talk about this topic, he was in the middle of a survival project, just like usual. He was up until midnight on a weeknight to bark-tan several deer hides to make his own shoes. "I could've just bought the leather, ya know? I've got a wife, two kids—one is a baby—and I'm just driven, just hooked to do it this deeper way." These hooks and pulls are what keep people coming back and going deeper into this world of survival.

For Dan, fire is such an important survival skill that he even wrote a book about it: *Ignite*. "Fire is such an old magical thing, such an old human invention. As humans, we have used fire to progress who we are. There is a deep, deep, ancestral psychological link between humans and fire." Even the word feels old to Dan, like some primordial Neanderthal language left over in modern English.

Fire ties into all major survival skills. It helps cook your food and keep you warm in your shelter. It's used to make tools, like fire-hardening a spear or burning out a bowl. It boils and purifies water or signals for help. "All of those things, fire enhances all of those things. It ties all of them together."

But for Dan, perhaps fire's biggest contribution is its psychological impact. "In a survival situation, fire provides hope and helps boost your attitude, especially if you are alone. Imagine being injured or freezing, being in that terrible dark space. Fire can be your tether to optimism and hope, which is ultimately the biggest thing and most important survival skill."

Important, indeed!

Survival Schools

While survival schools are now found all over the country and all over the world, that has not always been the case. In fact, there are a few key figures who played critical roles in popularizing survival skills and basically founding the movement. There are two well-known authors and teachers who are, in many ways, the grandfathers of the survival skills movement.

Larry Dean Olsen started a program at Brigham Young University in 1968 that started taking college students into the wilderness for 30 days to teach them resilience and adaptability. Olsen also wrote *Outdoor Survival Skills*, one of the first books on the subject. Olsen's BYU Survival Course would later evolve into the Boulder Outdoor Survival School in 1977 under the guidance of Olsen's senior students. BOSS is a hugely popular survival school with thousands of students having graduated from there over the years. It has been one of the leading edges of survival skills training and Stone Age–level living for over 40 years.

Around the same time, Tom Brown Jr.'s story and work began to take off. Tom had been mentored, trained, and partially raised by an elusive elder Apache man called Stalking Wolf in the Pine Barrens of New Jersey. Tom learned traditional survival skills, awareness, tracking, and also a deep spiritual approach from the man he called Grandfather. In 1978, Tom's book, *The Tracker*, was published and his Tracker School opened in New Jersey. Over the years, Tom has published over a dozen books and he has trained tens of thousands of students from all over the world in survival, tracking, awareness, and related fields.

Almost everyone I mention in this book is connected back to these two individuals and the schools and programs they started. In particular, many different people cited Tom Brown's books as a huge influence, in particular because many of the books contained stories giving life to characters enmeshed in the skills they were interested in and longing for.

In the 80s, one of Tom Brown's first and primary students, Jon Young, co-founded the Wilderness Awareness School with an elder named M. Norman Powell, aka Ingwe. Jon had grown up under Tom's guidance and mentoring, and Ingwe had grown up as a white man in Africa immersed with tribal groups, such as the Akamba, Zulu, and Bushmen, learning traditional survival skills and culture. WAS eventually moved to Washington State in the mid-90s, and it was there I started training and teaching. From the mid-90s on, WAS grew into one of the most prolific and extensive survival schools in the world.

In 1999, Jason Knight and I started the Wilderness Awareness Residential Program. This program would be the first 9-month survival immersion program in the world, and grew out of Jason's desire and vision to have a college-like survival program over the course of a year. Later, this program would be renamed the Anake Outdoor School. Jason would go on to start his own program Alderleaf Wilderness College. WAS would continue to grow both its youth and adult programs, eventually turning into a year-round school where people of all ages train in survival skills, deep nature connection, and cultural mentoring. Alderleaf would grow into the largest survival immersion school in the world. The 9-month survival immersion model has now been replicated all over the country and world.

There are numerous other survival schools all over the world. There is a major survival school in every bioregion in the United States, if not every state. Working with a local school and program is often the best first step if you are starting your own survival journey. Instructors often have expertise in local knowledge, flora, and fauna.

I'll let you in on a little secret: It's pretty easy for a skilled survival instructor watching a skill come to life on TV to tell if what he or she is watching is authentic or not. And, yes, reality TV does stage some of these moments. But this doesn't mean that staged survival skills are worse or better than others. Sometimes those staged experiences—that form the core of many shows—teach incredibly valuable lessons. But take away the camera crew and the producers and replace them with a lone subject who films himself or herself in the wild, like on shows such as *Survivorman* or *Alone*, and a rawness and rugged reality seeps through. Nicole Apelian is one of the core participants on the show *Alone*, and her performance on the show has been a huge inspiration to fans all over the world, especially women.

Nicole is a powerhouse of a woman. During her time on *Alone*, she spent 57 days completely alone in the Pacific Northwest wilderness on Vancouver Island. This is a huge amount of time to spend solo in the wild, even for experienced instructors. To give you some perspective, I am very proud of my own solo 5-day experience and a few other multiple-day solo experiences. Everybody I know that goes out to practice and hone their skills always takes at least one other person with them. Seeing someone go solo for 57 days practicing full-on survival is incredibly impressive, no matter how long you've been doing these things. Getting to pick Nicole's brain about being on television, and why she thinks people are so drawn to these experiences was very illuminating.

Survival-themed TV shows can be an escape for people from their normal day-to-day. It becomes an outlet or a way of escaping the doldrums of their lives. But, more importantly, Nicole believes we are subconsciously drawn to what we have done for tens of thousands of years.

"It's still in our DNA. We have only recently switched over from a hunter-gatherer lifestyle and it is what we somehow know." Many people are unhappy in their "modern" lives—it can be a lonely, stress-filled life—and survival TV offers an alternative way of living. And, per Nicole, some people do watch for the skills.

For the most part, people don't just end up on a survival skills show. They have to have some basic competencies, and, for the more realistic shows like *Alone*, participants often have to be experts. For Nicole, like for myself and many of the other folks featured in this book, survival and a deep connection to nature has been woven into her life from early childhood. We swapped stories about wild and free childhoods catching frogs and fish, building nature museums out of found objects, and exploring our own innate naturalist desires that were so common just a few decades ago but that are becoming increasingly rare.

Nicole told me stories of frequent nature adventures with her stepfather, who took her canoeing, dove deeply into field guides with her, and encouraged her collection of seashells and other nature objects. This early experience strongly piqued her curiosity, and she grew up in a household where her nest, seashell, and bug collections were not just tolerated but encouraged. Most survival skills instructors have similar experiences of a lot of solo nature experiences as children that set them up for success as an adult.

Nicole was gone for almost 2 months on *Alone*, and, ultimately, she decided to return because she felt her children needed her to come back. In today's era of being constantly connected and plugged in, what drives a person to spend 57 days alone away from society surviving on just her wits and skills?

Believe it or not, Nicole loved the challenge of *Alone*.

"I enjoyed the opportunity to be solo in the woods for 57 days. It was such a gift. Being out there alone was the highlight—my primal brain kicked in, and I felt a huge connection to all [of nature] around me. My brain and body felt switched on in a way that is not possible in daily living."

What happens when you start to awaken your primal brain and your ancient eyes awaken?

We shared an understanding of what this was like. The landscape becomes alive in new ways. The acts of making fire, boiling water, or simply sitting in the dark become deeply profound and meaningful.

For Nicole, much of her ability to enter into this space came from her time in remote parts of Africa. Not only is Nicole a survival expert, but she also has degrees in wildlife biology as well as a PhD in cultural anthropology. She has spent time doing remote wildlife studies deep in the bush and extensive time with tribal cultures, such as the Kalahari San Bushmen.

"I work with the Kalahari San Bushmen and [during the time on the show] I felt alive in a way I had, up until that point, only felt with them and when I lived solo in the African bush back in the 1990s. It was as if every neuron was firing and I could feel ripples of everything around me."

Nicole's unique experiences in the bush—like taking self-sufficiency to a whole new level by changing a tire next to a lion—really sharpened other vital survival skills, such as the ability to communicate and connect with animals and nature, track wildlife, and understand bird language. Staying tuned in to her surroundings was the foundational skill. These "soft" skills were the key to survival; if she didn't have them, she would have died.

Later, on Vancouver Island during the taping of *Alone*, Nicole drew on these skills again when encountering bears, cougars, and wolves. She spent time foraging with a male bear on the beach yards apart, and she was stalked by a cougar—twice. Even in the face of this, she felt calm, happy, and joyful, like being solo on that island was the most peaceful thing in the world. In fact, she could have stayed longer, and felt completely at home. She didn't feel lonely.

I echo Nicole's sentiments with my own experiences of encounters with large, wild animals, and how the interaction drops you into a deep, Zen-like reality. Thoughts float away when there are grizzlies around. Instead, you become fully present, senses tingling at max capacity, being 100 percent ready to take whatever action is necessary to survive.

All of this begs the question: Why are people drawn to these things in the 21st century, when we have all of our necessary creature comforts and support at home?

"I think a lot has to do with the lack of [having these deep, intrinsic connections] in the Western world," Nicole said.

"In a world where we are driven by production, rather than connection, many people are unhappy. This leads to physiological and psychological illness, as well. The internal drive for connection is strong and we, consciously or subconsciously, strive for it. Doing [survival] skills helps reconnect us to our primal selves and thus helps with happiness."

For Nicole, nature is the ultimate healer—for the mind and the body—and it is where we truly belong.

"We were not designed to live in nuclear households. Most people in Western culture are deeply unhappy," she added.

In her experience with indigenous cultures around the world, especially the Kalahari San Bushmen in Botswana, the norm was a connected community. People in these cultures were connected to self, others, and nature and, as a result, were deeply happy. But modern societies don't function in this way. We are so busy working, taking care of kids, and living indoors in our family bubbles that we have lost our connection to others. Perhaps primal connection through survival experiences is a medicine we all long for.

Survival skills are what our hands and bodies are naturally meant to do. They help tune us into our own DNA; after all, this is how our bodies are supposed to move. Practicing survival skills in a communal setting (like a school) brings an intergenerational village-like feeling to the experience, as well. These kinds of gatherings, where everybody of all ages and backgrounds can practice these skills together, are becoming more and more popular. "Skills bring us back to living as we are designed to live. In a village, we often have more of a purpose and feel happier and more alive."

We are all still hunter-gatherers in our physical bodies.

The impact of survival television shows on the primal movement cannot be overlooked in all of this. Many people have been inspired to explore herbal medicine and wilderness living skills as a result of watching shows like the one Nicole was on. For instance, since the debut of the show *Survivor* in 2000, followed up by shows like *Survivorman, Man vs. Wild, Dual Survival, Naked and Afraid,* and *Alone,* enrollment in survival skills programs for adults and kids rose over 100 percent and, in some places, over 1,000 percent in a 5- to 10-year period. This was reflected in the enrollment numbers I saw at the schools I worked at, and confirmed in schools all across the country and world.

Nicole's departure from *Alone* and her reintegration into modern society were difficult. "The transition back to society was very difficult, and I still don't feel as if I have fully transitioned (which I actually like). I now live in a home in the woods so I can be in nature all of the time." This sense of difficulty reintegrating into the modern world is something we all experience even from short periods of camping, backpacking, even going on vacation. How much more amplified must this be after spending nearly 2 months in a pristine, wild setting by oneself?

So, of her 57 days in the wild, what are some other lessons learned during that time that have stayed with Nicole? "The lack of technology while out there (no phone, no Internet, no social media) was super freeing. I also go on a media hiatus every time I travel or teach at a skills gathering (1–3 weeks at a time)—and every time it is such a blessing. Being away from the world pulling at you electronically is something I think we should all do more often. It lifts a huge burden."

It's almost as if our primal, hunter-gatherer brains rebel at the effects of our constantly plugged-in world. We will return to this theme again and again in this book, as, biologically and neurologically, there is something very interesting going on for all of us.

But let's go back to the specific survival skill of creating fire for a minute. Nicole spent 57 days with fire as her only source of light, heat, and cooking. What is it about fire that makes it one of the most coveted survival skills to master?

"Fire is key. It is water, it is warmth, it is food, and it is company. It is a skill everyone should master. I carry a lighter as well as a ferro rod (a small piece of metal that when struck forcefully produces a huge spark that can ignite in almost any conditions) and tinder with me 24-7 (as in *everywhere* I go). Having the skills to make a friction fire (with a bow- and hand-drill) is a great backup, but being prepared is even more important. That [being] said, getting fire by friction is an incredible primal experience."

But fire delivers more than simply practical necessities. For Nicole, some of the best conversations with her own kids occur when sitting around a fire, often simply staring into the flames and letting the conversation flow. (In fact, she often uses the act of sitting around a fire as a tool to resolve conflict in her family.) Fire makes for good storytelling. It creates a safe space for intimate ideas and feelings and wakes up something primal within us all.

Fire is the place we dance around, a place for rituals, trance dances, rhythm, and energy. It is our gathering space, a place where fire, food, and family unite. It's a place for freedom. "It's where we can let go of everything else. It's a place to let go of our phones, computers, and social media. It's a place for laughter, crying, and remembering who we are," said Nicole.

In many ways, hand-drill (another way of making friction-fire) is an advanced survival skill, but it's also likely the way we first learned to make and control fire. Evidence suggests that we started using fire at least 600,000 years ago when we weren't yet anatomically modern humans. Our first uses of fire were probably working with lightning strikes or wild fire and then capturing and containing the flame. However, at some point our ancestors figured out the magic of rubbing two sticks together and could make fire at will. This was an incredible act that forever changed who and what we are. In some way, all technology, especially technology that uses energy, is derived from discovery of how to make fire.

It took me years and years to get good at making fire. And the Pacific Northwest is a harsh mentor. The area is damp, cold, and sometimes extremely wet for up to 9 months of the year. It's actually an excellent place to hone one's survival skills. For years, I managed to just squeak out a bow-drill coal with lots and lots of effort, or I joined a team of people to make a hand-drill coal and contributed just enough to help a fire get started. On my solo survival trips, I always brought a lighter and matches (just in case).

A lighter is a very powerful tool. Tens of thousands of years of technology is condensed into a piece of plastic with metal and fuel that can produce life-saving fire for you in almost any context. I think most of us take that for granted. Lighter fires in hard, cold rain and after ice storms have saved my ass and my students' asses on more than one occasion. It's hard to comprehend the impact of this kind of technology on our journey as humans. What once took us millennia to master is now available to us in an instant. Taking a step away from this modern survival masterpiece, the lighter, to bow-drill is a step back in time and a step into our ancestral roots.

Being willing to go beyond bow-drill and make a fire by literally just rubbing two sticks together is an even further step.

If you think bow-drill is hard, hand-drill is definitely next level hard. To put it all in context, I only successfully created one solo hand-drill coal during my first extended 8 years of training and teaching in the Pacific Northwest. With a hand-drill, instead of using a piece of rope or cordage connected to a bow-shaped piece of wood to twirl your spindle back and forth, you have to use your own hands to spin a very thin piece of wood back and forth rapidly enough to cause ignition. And instead of using half of your body pressing down on a piece of wood to generate enough downward force, you have to use the muscles of your upper back, chest, and neck. It's very difficult to get your body weight involved, which, in contrast, is quite easy with bow-drill (there, you just lean in and press down with one hand).

When I moved to the Sonoran Desert for 4 years after leaving the Pacific Northwest, my fire skills blossomed. This is a common experience of people who spend so much time learning how to make fire in the soggy foothills of the Cascade Mountains. In other climates, it's actually dry a substantial part of the year, and it's not so difficult to harvest really good fire-starting materials. In the desert Southwest, I got better at hand-drill, harvesting the incredible combination of local seepwood spindles on desert spoon fireboards. Soon, I could get hand-drill coals regularly on my own.

This journey in many ways stretched back to when I was a teenager at ALI and extended into my stint as a survival instructor at WAS. Now, I was wandering and free in a new part of the world applying what I had learned. I felt a sense of accomplishment, connection, and independence. I was no longer tied to a lighter. Fire could come directly from the land around me. To celebrate this journey, I decided to do something I had never done before: make a special ceremonial fire all on my own. I decided to make a fire out of only materials I had harvested and gathered all myself.

This meant I couldn't use man-made cordage on a bow-drill. I wanted this experience to be different, special—a way of honoring fire. So, one afternoon I started gathering materials. I harvested dried and dead mesquite for fuel. I found patches of extremely dry grass and a little bit of cattail fluff for a tinder bundle. And I tuned up my own kit of seepwillow and desert spoon.

After building a solid tepee structure of mesquite, with an under layer of desert spoon shavings, I set down my tinder bundle and took out my kit. Before starting, I paused and gave thanks—thanks to the wood, thanks to the desert, thanks to the gift of fire, and thanks to the mystery beyond it all (perhaps to the fire gods themselves!). Then I cranked the seepwillow spindle back and forth in my hands while applying downward pressure. Smoke began to appear at the base of the spindle while I still had my hands at the top of the spindle (a thing I rarely experienced in my time in the Northwest). Images unfolded in my mind: the spider from John Five Bears story, the times I got fire when it was dumping rain, the first time I got a bow-drill coal, the times I saw my students get their first coal, and the times I had helped crank out a team coal on a dirt floor in the wintertime. After just a few passes, the hand-drill set was smoking, and I smelled the magic smell of combustion coming from the ignition between spindle and fireboard.

I slowly lifted my tinder bundle and flipped my newborn coal into it. Using my breath, I nursed it to life, and, as it burst into flames, I placed it in its home of sweet mesquite. The flame quickly spread, and, as the desert sun started to sink, the firelight flickered through the wash behind my home illuminating the prickly pear and barrel cactus. I felt something very special about that fire. I don't know why, but it really was different gathering and making everything myself. The flame flickered in its own magical rhythm, and the meaning behind this fire—and my creation of it—sunk in. I looked into the flames and remembered what it means to be human.

CHAPTER 2

The New Stone Age

Flint-knappers know that some stones break more evenly than others. . . . Obsidian has no crystal structure. Like a fluid, applied force spreads equally in all directions. . . . All flint-knappers, ancient and modern, know instinctively from endless trial and error how fine stone breaks.

—PAUL D. CAMPBELL,
SURVIVAL SKILLS OF NATIVE CALIFORNIA

THERE IS SOMETHING SO DEEPLY SATISFYING ABOUT MAKING stone tools. The first time I was exposed to the fine art of breaking rocks and making them into something cool I was in high school. My history teacher, Mr. Butler (or, as he liked to be called, "Mr. B."), was a gifted teacher. When teaching history, he roped us in with amazing stories, let us play historical role-playing games, and, perhaps best of all, dressed up in costume and read historical accounts while being disguised as a soldier from Alexander the Great's army or as a Medieval scholar.

He started the first day of the first class of history for all of us new students by bringing in small boulders of flint, putting on goggles, and then whacking the large pieces with an antler baton to get good-size chunks to work with. Next, he thinned those pieces with the antler or copper, and then proceeded to work those thinned pieces into incredibly beautiful and functional projectile points, or what most of us would call an arrowhead. It was a totally engaging and gripping way to hook your students on the first day of a class on prehistory and the evolution of human beings.

I had no idea of the impact and influence Mr. B would have on me and my life course. Mr. B. introduced me to the Ancient Lifeways Institute to spend time with his friend, John White (Five Bears), who himself took us much deeper on our Stone Age journey.

At ALI with Mr. B's class, I remember wandering the mostly dried up banks of the neighboring Kaskaskia Creek. There was a faint trickle of water down the middle of the creekbed that first summer. We splashed and played in the few places of deep water, and we pursued with delight the crayfish hidden under the large rocks. Along the banks there were deposits of clay where we would dig. We took the clay by hand and slowly shaped it into basic bowls for primitive pottery.

In my 13-year-old mind, we were just out for a fun adventurous creek wander. But after finding the right spot, we sat down as a class, and John proceeded to show us how we could take the rocks *all around us* and make our own stone arrowheads or projectile points. For me, this was some sort of fantasy come true. I had always desired to find an ancient Native arrowhead somewhere out in the wilds. I have no idea where this longing came from, just that I had wanted it for as long as I could remember. And, Five Bears was showing us how to make our very own.

Making projectile points out of chert (a hard, opaque rock) isn't easy, and our first efforts were pretty coarse. John, in a friendly, funny, and bantering way, would call us all up and look at what we had and present it to the group.

"What's this one for, picking your teeth?" he'd kid. "Is this some sort of stone comb? I think this one would bounce right off . . . even if it was a rabbit!"

This gentle mocking was a way of keeping us humble, and John offered technical pointers for us to work on. Many of us took away a deep appreciation of the sophistication that it takes to make stone tools. These were the kinds of tools that kept our ancestors alive and allowed them to feed themselves. These were tools and skills that were often called "primitive" but which took much more refined skill than we realize.

Later on, while teaching adults in the Anake program, I learned that you don't need to teach sophisticated rock-breaking skills for people to have fun, learn important skills, and get in touch with their more ancient selves. Rock-breaking day became one of my favorite days to teach. Every fall we took students out to an undisclosed location on one of the local rivers. There we selected a site with just the right combination of sand, rocks, and space, and we taught students to bash rocks.

This wasn't flintknapping, it wasn't rockwork, and it wasn't very sophisticated. We were making the most basic of stone tools. We were bashing rocks together hoping we would get a sharp edge of some sort. Mostly, students were breaking pieces of slate into basic edges to form a very primitive knife.

This was caveman stuff, straight out of Kubrick's film, *2001.* This was smashing and bashing to make our most original tools, and while it was not very sophisticated, it was super fun, useful, and exciting. This was about as *primal* as one could get. The tools we were making replicated basic stone hand axes that served as our ancestors' first-ever tools. Later in the day, students used these discoid "knives" or hand-axes they created to help carve a fire kit or to take down a willow sapling to make a primitive shelter or even to make a very basic bow.

After years of seeing how satisfying this is for people, I am still surprised. I go into the experience thinking that people won't want to break rocks or make stone tools or create survival shelters.

But people love it, and they dive in wholeheartedly to making shelters, breaking rocks, and making stone tools. I realized after some time that what is happening isn't a cerebral thing. It's not cognitive. What's happening is we are tapping into biology and neurology and how our brains are designed. We spent 200,000 years roaming the planet, making stone tools, and, somewhere locked inside our modern brain and body, we still want to.

I was exposed to the biological satisfaction of making stone tools as a teenager, and I've seen it come alive in others. But I'm only a fair to middling flintknapper at best. I love the practicality of knowing how to use stone tools to keep yourself alive, and I love taking people out and helping them break rocks to connect to their primal selves (and learn some useful survival skills). But there is a whole subculture out there of people who take this to a whole other level.

There is a modern Stone Age movement afoot. People are attending gatherings all over the world, dressed in buckskin or wool or furs, and learning the most ancient of skills. Their numbers are growing, and they have knowledge and wisdom to share with all of us, no matter how much time we want to spend on Instagram or Facebook.

For expert input and advice on Stone Age living skills, I first turned to Tom Elpel. Tom is the archetypal mountain man. He grew up mostly in Montana, wandering the forest, mountains, and meadows there as a child under the watchful eye of his grandmother. Tom's grandma passed on to him her knowledge of edible and medicinal plants, as well as a deep interest in survival skills.

Tom's grandmother kept a copy of Larry Dean Olsen's classic book, *Outdoor Survival Skills*, on the shelf. Larry was the founder of BOSS (see page 10), and his book is a classic in the field. Tom took a class at Tom Brown's Tracker School with his grandmother, proving without a doubt that he had the coolest grandma ever.

Tom is a strong, brawny man who built his own house by hand, which enabled him to escape the mortgage trap so many of us find ourselves in. He used his understanding of survival skills principles to build a passive solar stone and log house for "what most people spend on a new car." This simple living allowed Tom to pursue his dream of being involved in teaching other Stone Age skills through wilderness therapy programs and, eventually, his own school. Tom has written several books to date on everything from botany to survival skills to how to apply these principles to a modern life.

Tom and I have shared students over the years, and I respect his wisdom, experience, and understanding. I wanted to dig in with Tom and get his view on the importance of Stone Age living skills in the 21st century.

But, first, how do you define Stone Age living skills?

"Stone Age skills are whatever you want them to be. In a strict sense, that might entail discarding modern materials and technology, such as using stone and bone tools instead of steel to brain-tan hides and make clothing. However, Stone Age peoples tended to be practical-minded and would use the best tools available to them. If an arrowhead is needed, a glass bottle bottom will work as well as a natural, glassy stone."

Tom is fond of pointing out that he likes to do whatever works or whatever is practical rather than sticking to a perfect ideal. One of the first earth-lodges he constructed became unsafe because mushrooms started growing out of the rafters. He had to tear it down and chose to use slab wood waste from a local sawmill to rebuild the lodge. This practicality of "what works" is rampant throughout the survival skills world and is what allows people to make ends meet in a challenging field.

But if Stone Age living skills are "whatever you want them to be," what makes the difference between modern survival skills and Stone Age living skills? For Tom, it's pretty clear and simple.

"Modern survival skills largely rely on factory-made gear, such as space blankets, waterproof matches, fishing tackle, and guns. That's fine if your idea of survival is a credit card. Personally, I'm more interested in improvising with whatever is at hand— primitive or modern—to meet the basic needs for shelter, fire, water, and food."

With modern survival gear readily accessible and sold everywhere, from REI to Target, why is it, then, that Stone Age living skills are so popular at this time? Tom's answer echoed what many others have shared. "It could be argued that Stone Age skills provide a counterbalance to our increasingly technological world. The more wired everyone becomes, the greater the need to seek a balance and reconnect with the earth. However, I'm not convinced that's what it's all about."

Or, perhaps it's about leading a more passionate life. In an effort to remedy society's malcontent and disillusionment, Tom shares his passion for Stone Age living at gatherings like Rabbitstick Rendezvous. Started in the late 70s in Rexburg, Idaho, Rabbitstick Rendezvous is the oldest continuous Stone Age living skills gathering in the world.

Tom was an instructor at the first gathering, sharing his techniques for brain-tanning deer hides. This is a skill Tom learned from his cousin, Melvin Beatty, and Melvin is pretty much credited with reintroducing the skill of wet-scraping deer hides to the entire modern world. It's amazing to realize that someone could start making a living on a skill that had almost completely died out.

Stone Age Gatherings

In 1978, Larry Dean Olsen helped organize the first ever Stone Age technology gathering in the United States. The event was called Rabbitstick Rendezvous, and it would become the first of many similar gatherings. After, a few years, a name change, and some other people getting involved Rabbitstick gave birth to Wintercount, an annual winter gathering in the Arizona desert. In 1989, the Society of Primitive Technology was formed by a group of instructors to unite the growing fields of traditional, aboriginal, wilderness and primitive living skills. Many of the instructors in this and other chapters of this book have taught at Rabbitstick or other similar gatherings. Other prominent gatherings include Saskatoon Circle, Echoes in Time, Woodsmoke, and Rivercane Rendezvous.

These gatherings serve as amazing places to get an introduction to these skills; to see and understand the larger community of people practicing these skills; and to network with potential students, instructors, or schools. The gatherings are usually a week or two long and serve as a family-friendly mini survival-immersion for interested people.

In the late 90s and early 2000s, Peter Bauer, a student and teacher at these kinds of gatherings, developed a character or alter ego he dubbed Urban Scout. He used this persona to bring Stone Age skills to the streets of Portland through classes, public stunts, blogging, and writing while walking around wearing a loincloth and carrying a hand-drill kit. I would call Peter's work avant-garde, bleeding-edge Stone Age technology. Peter coined the term *Rewilding*, which has now become a popular term to cover Stone Age living skills, deep nature connection, and survival all rolled into one as a subversive movement challenging our current model for living. Peter now runs Rewild Portland, offering classes in these skills to a wide audience.

While tanning hides really isn't the survival skill I'm most passionate about, it is pretty wondrous to make leather out of hides discarded by hunters. Turning dead deerskin into buckskin that can then be made into clothes, pouches, cordages, bags, and other essentials is quite an eye-opener for most students. In fact, this skill was such a part of early American settler living that it informs the name of our currency. If you've ever referred to dollars as "bucks" (as in fifty bucks) you were referring to the time when tanned deer hides turned into buckskins were sold and traded for one dollar each. The slang stuck even into modern times.

If you ever want to learn how to make buckskin, attending a Stone Age gathering might be the way to go. The first gathering at

Rabbitstick started pretty small. Tom laughingly shared that there were fifty instructors and three paying students. But the movement has really grown. "Primitive skills gatherings are sprouting up all over the country as people discover not just a nature connection but also a tribal connection, a sense of belonging within a tight-knit community."

There are now gatherings like Rabbitstick happening in many different states and at many different times of year. These gatherings give you a crash course in stonework, making fire, tanning hides, making plant medicines, and dozens of other skills. Gatherings are almost as ubiquitous and popular as the modern music festival scene, and the two have started to blend in interesting ways as counterculture ideas and ways of life become popular in the festival scene. I've personally attended multiple music festivals where I was asked to share Stone Age skills and ceremonially open or close a festival with friction fire.

It's pretty amazing to see what happens when people start working with ancient tools and technologies, whether it's at a 9-month immersion program, a Stone Age gathering, or a modern music festival. You see this sense of wonder, bewilderment, and confusion often cross people's faces as they start to make something by hand, perhaps for the very first time.

But while it can be wonderful to see this transformation, it also highlights a sad reality about modern human life.

"Most people don't know how to use their hands beyond pushing buttons," Tom said. "To me, that's analogous to having a brain in a box on a shelf. What good is it if you can't do anything with it? To learn a new skill and create something, whether starting a fire by rubbing sticks together or tanning hides to make one's own clothes—now that's empowering. A skill begins with a thought or wish that lacks physical substance, yet is transmuted into reality through the hands. When you see people learn new skills, they are visibly empowered."

So why are these skills important at this time?

"We've lost touch with nature, and, in so doing, we've lost touch with reality," according to Tom. "We live in a world much like Plato's cave, where flickering firelight cast shadows of puppeteers on the wall as the only source of information about reality. In our case, we depend on the flickering lights of screens to inform us about the world, yet that information is useless without a physical connection to reality. The more time spent in nature, the more grounded one becomes."

We spend so much time not just inside but in front of screens. Recent research suggests that Americans spend between 10 hours to half of our waking time looking at screens, in a reality that is often abstract and constructed. It is very different than the reality of scraping hair and fat off a deer hide or of bashing stones together to make tools.

Tom sees this in his students as they begin to practice and learn basic skills.

"Building a shelter and collecting firewood helps quantify otherwise abstract principles, such as insulation, air infiltration, and fuel. You can physically feel the effects of insulation, feel any leaks that allow air infiltration, and measure the amount of fuel required to stay alive and comfortable. Learn to physically grasp these principles in primitive shelters, and you develop a basis to understand similar issues in a modern house or in national energy policy. That's essential if we hope to steward our natural resources wisely. Humanity would be doomed if people only learned about nature through computer screens."

Once people really get immersed in these skills, things change for them. They start to look at society differently. They become a third-person observer of what society can be like for some folks, and many choose to leave or pursue an alternative lifestyle.

Tom has done something similar in running his immersion program, Green University, and he applies these principles to his own life. Rather than have a big, expensive mortgage and lifestyle and then needing a job with a big salary and benefits to pay for it all, Tom has reversed things by building his own home and living off-grid, paying no mortgage or utility bills. This has allowed him to teach and write full-time and pursue his passions.

"Whether we live in a hut in the woods or in an apartment in the city, we all share the same basic needs for survival, such as shelter, warmth, water, and food. A survival philosophy can greatly facilitate life in the 21st century. Instead of getting a job and paying rent and other monthly bills, consider the shortest possible route to create or acquire decent shelter, warmth, water, and food. Having built my own low-cost passive solar home as a young adult, I've made a lifelong career out of not needing a job. When you take care of the survival basics, then you are free to do whatever else you want, and that's true regardless of whether you live in a cave or in a condo."

Next year, Tom plans on doing something he's never done before: leading a 6-month canoeing expedition with a dugout canoe he made himself. His goal is to spend 6 months on the river with his students. It's not a fully Stone Age level program, but people will be living simply, using their skills to remember a way of life so different than the rush of modernity that overwhelms so many of us so much of the time. This is the kind of journey that deep down inside many of us long for: 6 months of following the natural rhythms of water and sunlight; food together around a fire; and a band of people drawn together by a common goal and culture.

"The ultimate answer is that we don't have all the answers. We have to live our lives . . . I'm going to go paddle the river."

———

In 1991, on the border between Austria and Italy, two German tourists discovered a body of what they thought was a mountaineer. Little did they know that they had stumbled upon the oldest-to-date European mummy. Later dubbed "Otzi" after the location he was discovered in, this mummy was over 5,000 years old and was loaded with Stone Age gear. Though technically from the

Copper Age, analysis of Otzi, his gear, his health, and his apparent cause of death revealed stunning details about ancient Europeans and their lives.

Otzi is a big hit in the Stone Age living scene, and friends and colleagues of mine have tried to reproduce most of Otzi's gear and clothing. It's fascinating to read and hear about what he was carrying with him at above 10,000 feet to sustain himself in cold and ice. Otzi was covered in many different animal skins, wearing clothes from sheep, deer, bear, and cows. Even his shoes were made from different animal parts, including bearskin soles, deerhide side, and tree bark. Some scientists have speculated that his shoes were actually a form of ancient snowshoes and had detachable frames.

In addition, Otzi had with him a flint knife, a yew bow, a hazel-framed backpack, tinder made from fungus, and apparently some medicines to help treat his pain and possibly the case of intestinal worms he had.

While I haven't met anyone who's replicated all of Otzi's gear, and I certainly haven't tried myself, I think we could if we tried. Much of what Otzi wore and carried would still be damn useful today, especially in snowy mountains. The gear he wore is at least as useful as what I could get from REI or North Face, and quite possibly more so. The neck knife that Otzi carried is particularly intriguing as it is small but extremely functional. Some modern knife companies have now reproduced modern variations on it based off the basic functional blueprint of Otzi's knife. I've played with a few of these, and they are extremely useful and probably a better survival knife design than a great many of the bigger knives on the market. Bigger is not always better.

If there's somebody I know that dresses and carries gear like Otzi, it's Lynx Vilden. Lynx is a tall, blonde woman of European descent, who, when she's dressed in her gear, looks like she's walking out of the Stone Age. Lynx was inspired in her late teens by the book *Clan of the Cave Bear*, the Jean M. Auel classic story of the eclipse of Neanderthal culture by *Homo sapiens*. Lynx has been on a Stone Age journey ever since. Lynx is friends with Tom Elpel, who has joined her on some of her projects, and she has also taught at BOSS, Rabbitstick Rendezvous, and many other venues. She has studied and taught Stone Age skills for over 2 decades and has led multiple, multi-month Stone Age expeditions. On these "Stone Age Living Projects," Lynx takes students out on expeditions to remote areas using Stone Age gear and wild foods that they've all gathered and made themselves.

Lynx did a week of guest teaching at the Anake program when I instructed there. She started her week off by sharing a classic story about Crow stealing fire and then inviting us to help her get a hand-drill fire started. Lynx lit a cattail torch that had been soaked in deer fat and shared some stories of her adventures with the Stone Age Living Project. But it was Lynx's collection of handmade Stone Age tools and gear that left the most memorable impact on all of us that day.

Lynx had a bison skin sleeping bag with the fur on the inside. Having scraped bison hides as a teenager, I had a particular appreciation for the work and craftsmanship that went into creating this "primitive" sleeping bag. There were various gorgeous projectile points of obsidian, flint, chert, and other materials. Bone arrowheads, fish hooks, and scraping tools were another exquisite set. And, to top it all off, Lynx actually had a fossilized mammoth tooth toothpick—not something you could just pick up at REI.

Lynx spent the next several days teaching how to make bone tools from the lower legs of deer. This is a part that is discarded by pretty much all hunters, but we learned to make skin bags, rattles, bone knives, awls, and arrowheads. I was brought back to my ALI days by using a stone to scrape and wear away at the deer bone I was given. Once the bone is worn to a certain point, you lightly tap it over and over again with a rock to cause it to split in half and potentially into multiple pieces.

Lynx invited us to look at the pieces and see what was possible. What shapes were revealed by the way the bone broke? What did the bone want to be made into? This was how John White had taught. Despite having some interest in making a bone knife, after some examining of my bone fragments it became clear that a bone awl, a scraper, and bone arrowhead were the best possibilities. After Lynx's visit, one of the students became so enamored with bone work that she went on to create exquisite pieces of scrimshaw art out of bones she gathered and harvested over the years.

The bone tools I made with Lynx are still around and they fit comfortably next to clay bowls from ALI or track casts from WAS wolf-tracking expeditions. While my collection of tools and objects is never going to reach the sophistication of Lynx's, it serves to remind me of powerful and important experiences. My tendency to build a "nature museum" of these mementos is probably also an echo of ancient ways of tracking and telling stories that people have engaged in.

While Lynx's teaching style, visit, and gear fit right in with WAS and the Anake program, it's important to note that in general Anake is a blend of ancient and modern and teaches all styles of survival. While it may have been the first long-term survival immersion program in the world, it's now just one of many. There are many different schools out there with different "flavored" immersion programs now, from the aforementioned Green University to Jason Knight's Alderleaf Wilderness College. However, there's only one full-on Stone Age survival immersion program out there, called Teaching Drum Outdoor School, and it's run by a man named Tamarack Song.

If interviewing Tom Elpel is connecting with the archetypal mountain man and talking to Lynx is like speaking to a character out of a Jean M. Auel book, then talking and spending time with Tamarack is like spending time with Gandalf or Dumbledore from the beloved Harry Potter series. He's the archetypal wizard sprouting a bushy white beard and spouting useful advice and wisdom nonchalantly at will. Even his name evokes something epic, storybook-like, and from another era.

Tamarack's expertise lies in Stone Age living skills, deep nature connection, and survival, and he's written several books about it. I first became a fan of Tamarack's work 15 or so years ago when I read an article he wrote about the advantages of moccasins over shoes (something we'll look at in the next chapter). Reaching out to Tamarack to discuss this topic was a great excuse to get to know a true elder in this field.

Tamarack runs the Teaching Drum Outdoor School in central Wisconsin. Teaching Drum grew out of Tamarack's desire to start an intentional community based around Stone Age living. The school is one of the oldest in the country, and it has one of the most intense and immersive survival skills programs around. I've heard stories of students who were in his *11-month* immersion program (the longest I know of and have heard of) being thrown a deer carcass and rocks to create their meals for *multiple weeks*.

Tamarack is passionate about sharing his knowledge with others. In his words, "Giving is receiving. This is something I learned from the elders. Fresh wine is to be enjoyed, holding it back turns it to vinegar."

See? Very Gandalf.

So, in this world of modern luxury and comfort, not to mention REI and North Face, how does one first get into the world of Stone Age living and survival? Tamarack shared his story with me. Turns out, it started with his mother.

Tamarack's earliest memories of picking wild strawberries with his mother started before he was 3 years old. Tamarack's mom grew up in the Depression era, and foraging for wild foods wasn't an option, it was a necessity. His mother also gathered hazelnuts on their way to school to supplement the lard-and-bread sandwiches they'd often eat when no other food was readily available for the family. These early foraging skills woke up something deep in Tamarack, and they continue to serve him to this day.

His mom isn't doing too bad either.

"Mom is 89 and still healthy. She still gathers food by picking day lilies from her yard and even gleaning food from the fields after the farmers have picked their crops," he shared.

These early foraging experiences shaped Tamarack's desires, interests, and passions. Tamarack sees this foraging and gathering instinct alive in many people these days and not just in his survival immersion students.

"It's all in our blood. It's in our genetic heritage. It's what we are drawn to. Just look at how people go to the supermarket. We are still foraging," he pointed out.

Tamarack was not the only person who shared with me the parallels between shopping and gathering activities of subsistence hunter-gatherer communities. Could it be that our instincts to buy food, clothes, and other items is a genetic tendency inherited from our ancestral roots? This is something I've thought about and questioned in my own life and have brought up to my family and friends.

For Tamarack, it's not just our shopping tendencies that reveal our Stone Age longings. During our discussion, Tamarack linked everything from finding our keys when they are lost to getting across town to watching action movies and murder mysteries to our innate hunter-gatherer tendencies. "There's something there that defines what it means to be human. We are manifesting it all the time, no matter what the patina or surface. Peel that off and what's there? The essential human."

These instinctual longings even spread into our choice of recreation and free time. What kinds of things do we do with our vacation time? Go to the beach or the lake or the mountains. We take risks by going kayaking or skiing or backpacking or hiking. We get back to the primal wild whenever we can regardless of whether we are rich or poor.

Like many people in this book, Tamarack immersed himself fully in these longings after a childhood full of deep nature connection experience. Catching frogs, snakes, and even pigeons created a deep empathy for him with all wildlife. When Tamarack would come home from school, he'd change his clothes and then run out into the freedom of the forest, creeks, and fields near his house. Outside he would gather elderberries, build forts, catch animals, and even build rafts to float in the nearby swamp. It's amazing how children, when left to themselves, will innately practice these hunter-gatherer skills.

Tamarack took his naturalist intelligence and empathy into the field of wildlife conservation when he went to college. However, after a few years Tamarack realized that the classes he was taking and the field he was in wouldn't allow him the deep connections he longed for.

"I didn't want to do deer censuses. I didn't want to be a researcher or bureaucrat," he reflected.

I've heard this same sentiment from students and colleagues of mine for years. Many of them land at a survival skills immersion program after a background in wildlife research (like Nicole Apelian), but they find that the overly scientific approach, the constant data-collecting, and analysis robs their experience of wildlife and nature of wonder and magic.

Many of the people in this field are also wanderers at heart. Lynx has traveled all over North America teaching in various places. As you'll see in the next chapter, wandering may be a core human practice harkening back to our nomadic ancestry. Tamarack is not an exception to this rule. He left college and started the journey that would give him the skills to realize his dreams. He spent quite a while hitchhiking across the country seeking to find elders in the Native American community who could teach him the old skills and ancient ways. Tamarack apprenticed himself to whoever would accept him in these communities and spent time learning from Hopi, Blackfoot, Ojibway, and Lakota elders. Tamarack deepened his physical skills as well as his cultural and spiritual understanding. It was around this time that he was given his name by a Native elder.

One of the things that Tamarack noticed in his travels in the Native American community was that the cultures he spent time in didn't have a word or even concept for nature. "There wasn't any separation from nature . . . your living room was nature."

Teaching Drum was founded as a nonprofit school. It's designed to help Tamarack and his teaching team share these kinds of skills and understanding with interested seekers. As people become more disillusioned with society's high levels of consumption or its overly social media–focused culture, they sought out teachers like Tamarack.

What it comes down to is people fulfilling an age-old search for self.

Simply put, there's too much information coming at us every minute of every day. People need and want something simpler, and seeking out their ancient roots provides that for them. And a lot of the challenges happening in today's society are driving people toward this simpler way and time.

"So much is not working in contemporary society," Tamarack said. "All of our sacred institutions are failing: the church, our educational system, marriage, and especially politics. Going back to basics, this is what we want—our yearning for mystery, intrigue, and adventure. This is why survival skills are so alluring . . . why there are all the reality shows and survival skills show. It's really about what it means to be human."

So why is it important to learn these skills at this time? What value do these ancient skills have for us in our contemporary society?

"We have become so intellectually and cerebrally oriented," Tamarack stressed. "We have bodies but we don't know how to use them, and we now have diseases that our Stone Age ancestors never had, like rampant obesity and diabetes. Stone Age skills bring it right back to the body. It has to do with tools. For Stone Age people, the ultimate tool is your body."

Tamarack echoed what Dan Corcoran had shared earlier; the ultimate survival level is to be able to walk into nature with just the clothes on your back, or even naked, and literally make everything you need by picking up stones and sticks. I thought about the strange visceral satisfaction of making stone arrowheads on the banks of Kaskaskia Creek at ALI or of making a bone awl with Lynx.

"We are a tool species," said Tamarack. "Other animals use tools and manipulate their environment, but for humans our niche is to use tools that are an extension of our hands and eyes. . . . It's very valuable to go back to basics, to go back to what it is to have and use a stone tool."

Tamarack, ever the Zen-wizard, had some final words of wisdom to impart:

"Rather than observe, move. We are passive in our society, so sedentary. Go out and walk around, allow everything to become three-dimensional. In order to find this three-dimensional perspective in nature, we have to move."

And, "Be rather than do and immerse yourself. . . ."

Gandalf, indeed.

My times with Tom, Tamarack, and Lynx revealed and ripened a lot of memories from my time at ALI, and one story that had been dormant for years re-emerged.

At ALI, we did a lot of different activities, including Stone Age living skills and crafts such as using atl-atls (ancient spear-throwers), flintknapping, processing of animal hides, and making primitive pottery. However, we also did plenty of activities that were designed to help us grow and stretch in other ways that weren't necessarily hard, technical Stone Age skills.

One of those activities was a giant awareness game called Raiders and Refugees. Half, or sometimes more than half, of the students were designated as "refugees." This group was taken to an undisclosed location in the forest nearby. Its goal was to make it back to camp unseen by any of the rest of us (the "raiders"), who were tasked with capturing them. To capture them all we had to do was see them. If we saw them, they were automatically captured. Sounds easy, right?

I loved this game, and it was super fun, engaging, and exciting. It got us out of our focus-mind brain, and expanded our awareness of the forest and the surrounding hills. The only problem was I sucked at it. Not only did I suck at it, but all of us "raiders" sucked at it. For whatever reason, I always ended up being a raider (perhaps John Five Bears had some obtuse lesson he was trying to teach me), and after 6 years, none of us had ever captured a single refugee. Not one. The refugees, led by two of John Five Bears' sons, Watie and Jonah, seemed to always find a route that eluded us time and time again.

One of my last times at ALI, I was once again stuck being a raider, and I vowed that this time would be different. Often, as raiders, we moved around through the edges of the forest trying to find the refugees. Every time we did this, we made a lot of noise, and Jonah or Watie simply read the corresponding disturbance in the birds and animals and knew where we were. So, my strategy this time was different. I would find a quiet place on the edge of the forest and sit still out of sight, waiting and listening for any sign of the refugee players.

As I walked toward the southern edge of the property where there was a fence line border, I found myself way more relaxed than I had been when previously playing the game. I calmly meandered along the fence line and found a sweet spot where I could sit and rest against a tree, unseen. The spot was on the hillside in the forest near the fence, but with cover on at least three sides. I could stay comfortable and quiet for a long time there. Or, at least, I hoped I could.

Sitting on the hill, I listened to the play of bird songs and sounds and watched the leaves shimmer in the breeze. It was easy to fall into a trance or daydream while there. I didn't have any idea how long I had to wait, and time seemed to just melt into timelessness.

At some point, I found myself thinking about flintknapping. I thought that this would be a cool spot to sit and do some stonework. That thought kept fading in and out of mind for a while, while my eyes lazily wandered over the landscape around me. At some point, I spotted some stones embedded in the loose soil in front of me. I quickly became curious and started to remove the three chunks of chert.

The soil was quite loose and light, and my excitement cranked up. I soon realized that I was holding three pieces of chert that looked like they had been broken apart deliberately in an attempt to make stone tools.

I couldn't believe it! I had always wanted to find an arrowhead out in the field somewhere, and while these weren't arrowheads, I was holding in my hands chunks of rocks that looked to me like they had been worked on by an ancient person a long time ago. I was stunned and in a daze. Suddenly, I heard a disturbance up the hill. I slowly slunk back into the shadows of the tree, and, 2 minutes later, one of my fellow students came down the hillside following the fence line. Busted! I had captured my first refugee.

The two of us made our way quickly back to camp to share my discovery with John, Watie, and Jonah. John and Watie examined the chert for a few minutes. Finally, John spoke:

"Well . . . ya know, it's probably best to leave these kinds of things at the place we find them. Keeping them in the ground helps us understand more about what's going on. But these sure do look like someone was making stone tools."

"You can also see here where the rock was obviously heat-treated. That's used to make chert easier to work with. Someone must have had a fire up there a long time ago," added Watie.

John double-checked to make sure that none of the family members had been doing rockwork up at that location before. It was soon confirmed that we had discovered artifacts that were hundreds or possibly thousands of years old. I was elated, mystified, excited, and filled with wonder and awe.

I don't know exactly what happened that day. I'm not sure it's important to figure that out. I do know that, mysteriously, I had bumped up against a different time and place through the wonder of stone and the art of making stone tools. Somehow the past had collided with the present, and I was lucky enough to be in the middle. When I think of what value learning ancient living skills hold for us, I am reminded of this experience. I hope that others get a similar taste of connecting to their ancient and primal nature.

CHAPTER 3

Wild and Primal: Thriving Through Natural Movement

If we go back on our four legs and get down on the ground, we may be able to do things we had no idea we could do.
—DR. GORDON SHEPHERD, NEUROSCIENTIST,
QUOTED IN *NATURAL BORN HEROES*

WE WERE TRUDGING UP THE HILL, AND WE WERE PROBABLY whining. Jonah and Watie were taking us all on a nature hike to explore the woods nearby. Up at the top embedded in the forest was a partial replica of a stone Celtic hill fort, so at least there was a cool destination. But our somewhat out of shape, soft suburban teenage bodies were complaining as we navigated the rocky, rugged uphill trail.

Looking back, the trail was actually pretty gnarly: loose scree, big rocks, rough roots poking out, and a pretty decent grade. But I'm sure our slow pace and complaining were exaggerated in comparison to the actual hardship. It's no wonder that Jonah and Watie decided to pull out a trick to get us moving.

"All right everybody . . . race to the top. We'll even give you a 15-second head start. GO!!!!"

We may have been lazy, soft, suburban teens, but we were still teens full of bluster and ego. We responded to Jonah's challenge by starting to run up the hill. However, the trail was so rugged that we literally stumbled into each other. The ground was uneven, hard, and awkward, and it certainly made me feel awkward and clumsy. Even with our 15-second head start, we hadn't made it very far up the steep grade.

I nearly lost my mind when a few seconds later Jonah and Watie sprinted past us, leaving us in the literal dust, and raced to the hilltop with ease. It took the rest of us a while to catch up to them, and we were all deeply winded. Several of us had bruised shins and almost everybody was dusty and dirty.

I couldn't believe how easily Jonah and Watie had beaten us, and even more unbelievable was how effortless they had made running uphill look.

Later, after we had explored the hill fort and then had a pretty epic solo sit in the forest, I asked Jonah, "How did you do that?"

We were just coming back to the crest of the hill, and we were about to head downhill.

"Nate, you don't think Watie and I were actually running on the trail do you? Look about 2 feet to either side of the trail."

I glanced at the spot Jonah pointed to. On either side of the trail, the ground was flat, even, and had a light layer of old leaves and detritus. The trail we had been on was clearly the drainage off the hill and was filled with all manner of awkward obstacles.

Jonah and Watie had simply let us charge forward up the middle of the wash, and then, after we stumbled over each other, they had leaped to the side of the trail and then dashed past up the hill. ALI wasn't just about learning skills like flintknapping and fire-making. This kind of moment also included a healthy dose of awareness training.

Seeing Jonah and Watie run up the hill that day made me want to be able to do the same, and it would become a core part of my teaching style to help free people from the constraints that civilization places on their bodies. Not only would I be able to do things like that, but I would help everybody do the same.

⸻

When most people hear the term *survival*, certain images and qualities come to mind: things like fire-making, hunting, purifying water, making shelter, and gathering wild food. However, survival encompasses a much broader set of skills and awareness than most people realize. Being a survival skills instructor meant that we all had to be good in the core competencies: survival, tracking, bird language, plant studies, leadership and communication skills, and being a good naturalist. But over time, we all developed passions and specialties, and topics we loved to teach about. For me, some of my favorite days to teach were our Natural Animal Movement days.

These days of class combined awareness training with an elaborate set of physical and mental exercises that Jon Young, the founder of Wilderness Awareness School, had developed with his friend, Lyle, many years ago. The exercises combined stalking and movement skills from Jon's studies with Tom Brown and Lyle's own studies of Chinese martial arts, including Tai Chi, Bagua, and Xingyi. The fusion of these two practices created a series of exercises that not only served as a way to loosen and limber the body and keep it in good shape, but were a key to rewilding our body and helping us to travel freely over any landscape.

One way of understanding what these natural animal movements were all about is to consider the popularity of yoga or Crossfit. Yoga classes have become so popular and widespread these days that almost everybody has attended a class, and a lot of folks attend classes regularly. But what really happens in a yoga class? One way of breaking it down is to realize that people spend at least 50 percent of a yoga class on all fours or some variation of all fours in poses named after animals, such as Downward Dog, Cobra Pose, Dolphin Pose, Pigeon Pose, and Eagle Pose.

Similarly, in Crossfit classes some of the classic moves, such as Burpees or Mountain Climbers, are highly aerobic, challenging movement done on all fours, and, in many classes, participants regularly do an exercise called Bear Crawling, where they crawl around the room on hands and knees for extended periods of time. Getting down on all fours and getting us out of our regular movement patterns is apparently really good for our health.

One of my favorite days of teaching natural animal movement at the Anake program occurred about two-thirds of the way through the school year when there happened to be about 6 inches of snow on the ground. That day, we had left a note for students at our usual meeting site with instructions to join us at the Jedi Training Center. No, really, that's what it's called: the Jedi Training Center (I didn't name it, but I sure as hell enjoyed the name). They were to come find us, get a fire going (to help warm us due to the snow and high level of damp cold air), and then we would have our third Natural Animal Movement day at that site. Just finding us and getting the fire going on top of snow would be excellent training and set the tone for a powerful day.

One of my jobs for that day was to embed and hide myself at the location before the students got there to help pique their awareness. This kind of thing was one of the really fun aspects of the job, and one that many of my fellow instructors enjoyed as well. Of course, on that day I was cold and uncomfortable, and I had to lay hiding for at least 45 minutes on top of snow crammed underneath a sword fern to pull it all off. My layers of wool camouflage kept me warm, and I tried to sink into a quiet place as I endured the cold. The look of wonder, excitement, and amusement on the students' faces when I popped out to join them after they had the fire going was totally worth it.

As we gathered around the fire, I had the task of not just teaching the core curriculum of the day, but also motivating everybody to be excited about crawling on their bellies through the cold snow. To accomplish this, I told them a few stories about applying natural animal movements in real life situations, and I could feel at least a little excitement beginning to mount.

To prepare ourselves we did a series of mobility warmup exercises, all based on animals and our creative imagination. Again, there are some parallels to something like a Crossfit class done in the woods, as mobility and joint rotation have become a key part of fitness across the country these days. We used moves like Deer Scrapes Antlers (where we do a full spinal circle forward and backward with our head and neck) and Hummingbird Hovers in Front of Flower (which involves imagining our arms as hummingbird wings and rapidly rotating them in circles at the elbows). Our bodies and minds both began to awaken more deeply and warm up more fully. We continued with moves to loosen our backs by imagining we were bears rubbing against a tree, and limbered up our core by rotating our waist and spine in circles and spirals with Otter Dives Deep—visualizing ourselves swimming through a river. Being fully warmed up, it was time to get to work.

Over the next 45 minutes we reviewed the core animal movements we had learned before, including Fox-Walking, Coyote-Running, Deer-Bounding, Bear-Lumbering, and other all-four forms, including Raccoon Form, Cougar Form, Bobcat Form, Side Monkey, and a couple of landing forms, such as Cat Landing and Owl Landing. These exercises cover core human movements, such as running, jumping, crawling, and hiding, but they also have parallels to what you might see in a kids' gymnastics class.

Getting students to literally crawl on their bellies on frozen ground is by no means an easy task. While people might do similar exercises to what we were doing in a Crossfit or yoga class, doing them in the forest and on the snow made it almost like doing a mini Tough Mudder race. I took the approach I often did as an instructor to help motivate people: by leading from the front. As we progressed into Salamander Form, Gecko Form, Mole Form, and even the face-planting Slug Form, I demonstrated each of the forms first for the students, and then proceeded to do the forms with them. Embodying the wild and vital qualities you hope to awaken in your students goes a long way to getting them to jump in with full participation.

Sitting around the fire for lunchtime, we shared our experience of what it had been like to practice natural animal movement on snow and in cold conditions. Students definitely mentioned the cold and discomfort, but many of them also spoke of becoming really present, being fully in their senses, and feeling their thinking, talking mind disappear at least for a little while.

After lunch we gathered for one final exercise. Students were to pick an animal and then spend at least an hour wandering, traveling, and experiencing the landscape as much as they could through the eyes of that animal. The only instruction was to hold the image of that animal strongly in their imagination, in their mind's eye, and then do what felt natural.

Watching all the students depart, it was incredible to see the changes that had happened to them since they had started the year. It was amazing to see how different they moved even compared to that morning. Gone was the stiffness that we had all brought to that early winter morning. Everybody's weight was more sunk into their feet, and they were moving fluidly with and around obstacles. They were playful and alive and vibrant with their steps through the sword ferns, and those that were on all fours were beginning to look comfortable with it, rather than awkwardly straining. It was quite the sight to see so many people disappear into their animal selves and literally dance with the landscape.

Over the last 10 to 15 years, there has been a seismic change in the exercise industry. As we have become more and more aware of the damages and dangers of a sedentary lifestyle and the perils of too much chair- and screen-time, a radical band of pioneers have been transforming how we exercise. They have been literally rewilding our bodies through such disciplines as barefoot running, parkour, Earthgym, natural movement, and animal forms training. I've had the fortune to cross train with and interview experts in these fields as I've continued my own journey of natural primal movement.

One of the first places to start on this journey is with your feet, literally. Barefoot walking and running is now a huge field and industry that peaked in sales in 2010 at $1.7 billion, and we even have the ironically entitled "barefoot shoes" as a brand. And, while I love barefoot shoes and have a few pairs, there really is something to walking around and connecting to the earth with bare feet. I've been doing it for years, both solo and with students. There's now considerable science to back up the practice of walking barefoot on the earth as a therapeutic exercise. In the book *Earthing*, authors like Stephen Sinatra, MD, who specializes in anti-inflammation treatments, show that when we put our feet on the ground, a natural anti-inflammation and anti-pain process starts through changes in the electromagnetic field of our bodies. NFL teams like the Seattle Seahawks now incorporate this into some of their routines by walking barefoot on the football field at the end of practice.

If you want to really understand why you might want to spend a lot of time barefoot, or if you want to explore ways of training your body in nature in a completely new and different way, Mick Dodge is one of the best resources. Mick, sometimes known as the Barefoot Sensei, is a wild, fun, and sometimes pretty hilarious character with his own television show. He's also kind of my father-in-law.

I met my wife, Karen Joy Fletcher, swinging hammers—the stone, iron, and steel variety modeled after ancient maces from Northern Europe—at a workshop with Mick. Karen's been one of Mick's core students for over a decade and is his "adopted daughter." Imagine twirling and whirling a 20- to 35-pound weight in the air around your head and body for several minutes at a time until you have to let it go from near exhaustion. This was just one of Mick's many training tools that I learned about over several years. Before meeting Mick, I considered myself pretty well-versed in ways to move wildly and effortlessly through a natural landscape, but Mick opened my eyes to a completely different way of finding physical vitality through vigorous exercise in nature: Earthgym, his synthesis of exercise, philosophy, movement, and connection honed through decades of training in snowy mountains, rocky river beaches, deep mossy forest, and up and down the West Coast of America.

Mick's approach, ideas, and stories are epic, even legendary, and they match his personality: a startling blend of backwoods, blue-collar, hard work, and highbrow earth-based philosophy, poetry, and song. Seeing Mick is like seeing a character out of a Tolkien novel; he wears elk hide tunics, wool leggings, and kilts. He is almost always barefoot, revealing tattoos across his feet resembling the roots of trees. A colleague of mine remarked that Mick had a very particular dwarfish look about him, referring to his very strong, dense muscular build and huge, bushy white beard.

Mick is the self-styled "Barefoot Sensei," and he has had his own wildly popular television show on National Geographic entitled *The Legend of Mick Dodge*. The title wasn't his idea, and he doesn't like it much. Over the years of training with Mick in the Hoh rainforest or in other parts of Cascadia, I heard him say the show was a great opportunity to connect with a large audience to get his message across, but he didn't like what the producers and writers expected of him. Often, they wanted him to say or do absurd or ridiculous things that weren't realistic. Eventually, Mick started to refer to himself as the stunt-double for the guy they were trying to portray on television.

Training with Mick, regardless of situation or circumstances, allows Mick's philosophy of movement, life, and earth to come out, and it is both very simple and very profound. What is this core philosophy? How does Mick sum it up? He answers with a simple saying: "Follow your feet and the earth will teach. And your feet will show you what you seek."

Within this saying is Mick's desire to get everybody out of their shoes and to let their feet feel a connection with the earth, the soil again. This is one of the simplest ways to pursue our own primal nature. He sometimes refers to himself as a "barefoot shoe salesman," trying to get people to feel and remember how good it can feel to be barefoot.

I've seen time and time again when adults, kids, even elders come completely alive in a new way after they remove their shoes and walk on bare ground. They light up as they feel the sweet coolness of gentle, dewy moss underfoot or begin to giggle at the slippery, succulent feel of mud on the balls of their feet and creeping between their toes. It's almost like they're being reborn, or something that was forgotten is remembered. Smiles, wonder, and delight permeate people's faces as their nerve-endings in their feet come back to life and send new signals to their brains. It also awakens some core ancestral way of living and being with the earth and with their bodies.

Also embedded in the saying is Mick's idea of wandering and living a nomadic lifestyle. This is in contrast to our overly sedentary modern-day lifestyle. Mick likens spending too much time in chairs, looking at screens, and being sedentary to the highly refined dietary evolutionary mismatch of white sugar.

"Thousands of years ago . . . every once in a while you come across sugar. Now, technology made it so we eat a couple hundred pounds a year. Something similar has happened with our bodies. It doesn't have to be that way. Walkable cities and communities are possible. Why do we make so many places [where] we can't walk barefoot?"

Mick often encourages people to take their challenges, their questions, and their inquiries for a run. The act of putting one foot in front of the other over and over again on the earth helps create new insights, new awareness, and is the basis for many of Mick's ideas.

He pointed out to me, "For millions of years our species [had to] run, gone on foot to eat and not be eaten. So, to me, no matter what habit you are stuck in, no matter what thinking is chewing at you while sitting, take it for a run and run until you can run no more, and then start running until you start dancing it out of the moment."

I've taken this practice out to the forest, mountain, river, and hills myself, and I've encouraged my students to do the same. It's amazing what comes to you when putting a question out to the universe and then moving through a wild landscape. Maybe it frees our unconscious to more deeply chew on an issue. Maybe Mother Nature gives us an answer or perhaps something in-between. No matter what the case is, it works. Problems untangle, and new thoughts and ideas emerge. We discover a primal connection and perhaps new answers.

"[People] learn to move differently and connect, and each person is different," according to Mick. "There are some common structures that we share as humans and animals, but each person moves in their own way, have their own reflexes, reactions, and reflections, which are the three cornerstones of forming a habit in a habitat."

One of the biggest modern-day challenges we humans face is our propensity to sink into boredom and laziness and to ignore our curiosity. For Mick, curiosity is what gets him going outside. My wife, Karen, also speaks frequently of the curiosity that pulls her and her students outside, and I must admit that having my curiosity piqued gets me out the door as well. For Mick, the curiosity is often about pain or cold or heat, about our limits. He encourages us to get "out of the insulation" of our houses and our devices. "Too much control of my environment weakens me."

This is the drawback of the luxuries of modern life. Too much time in front of the computer, coupled with too much time in a temperature-controlled environment, makes us reluctant to face the elements: to feel the heat or coolness of the air, to feel the rain on our faces, and to feel the wind blowing through the air. But when we follow our curiosities and venture again outside, soon the discomfort of a changeable environment becomes pleasant and even welcome. We rediscover our primal human strength and endurance. Cold, heat, wet, dry, and even dark become friends and teachers helping us find inner and outer strength, resilience, and fortitude.

Strength is another core part of Mick's philosophy. Under his tutelage and with Karen's guidance, I've discovered completely different ways of playing with nature and wild landscapes that have taken me beyond the animal forms movement I had pursued and practiced for so long. A key component of Mick's Earthgym approach is finding "tools" to play, dance, and train with. These tools include rocks, sticks or staffs, ropes, and hammers—all while making sure we remember to be barefoot, alive, and spontaneous.

Earthgym's staff or stick training involves using large, thick straight pieces of wood about the same height as yourself, or a little shorter. The sticks are used to move through a variety of mobility exercises called "open branch." Next, you plant one end of your staff in the ground and you can use the staff as a leverage point to stretch, tone, and strengthen the body through a series of yoga-like stretches called "planted branch." Finally, you can take your training to actual trees, doing a series of hanging exercises, swings, and climbing called "rooted branch." All of these "exercises" are done with a spirit of spontaneity, freedom, and play. The effects have been marvelous in myself, my colleagues, and my students. Mick equates stick training to when we swung in trees as our primate progenitors. He speculated that when we came down out of the tree, we quickly picked sticks up as a form of comfort and remembrance of our time living in trees. I think he's onto something.

Rock training is another favorite part of Earthgym and another powerful tool to build strength, resiliency, and at the same time release deeper emotions that may be blocked. Again, the emphasis is on your own creativity, play, and spontaneity, but the opportunity is to train with various-size rocks through a series of circles, waves, and spirals. You can train using one small rock in each hand and whirl the hand in circles to open the joints, relax the tendons, and prepare the body for heavier work. Next, you can move up to swinging medium-size rocks, one in each hand. Eventually, you can use a heavy medium-size rock to go through more waves and circles. Then there's big rockwork.

While all of this may sound a little bit like CrossFit or high-intensity interval training done in a forest (which it certainly is to some extent), working with heavier rocks starts to unfold ways in which people can use Earthgym to go deeper and release stuck emotions. Rockwork allows people to move through a lot of confusing emotions, old traumas, or deep things holding them back. People often respond by spontaneously crying, erupting in waves of joy, or breaking out in elation as they release whatever has been plaguing them through rock training. It's a very effective cathartic letting go: holding a heavy rock above your head while working through a painful memory, or swinging a heavy rock as you work through a belief that no longer serves you, and then spontaneously letting it all go as you throw your rock, your muscles approaching full fatigue.

Karen and I recently took this teaching method up to Soaring Eagle Nature School in Vancouver. With only an hour or so of this kind of training, several key Soaring Eagle school staff had pivotal transformational experiences in the woods just on the northern edge of the city. I've also recently discovered that there are still lingering traditions of ancient stone-lifting and stone-training practices in Scotland and Iceland. This is clearly documented in the Netflix series *Strongland* which features the history of these practices as well as their use by current Crossfit champions and world-class power-lifters.

It's widely acknowledged that our modern lifestyles are far more sedentary than our ancestors. So how do we remedy this?

"What is the remedy? What is the cure? I have no idea other than to step out of the insulation, develop a practice of doing so, and seek the cure, be curious," Mick suggested. "The Buddha spoke to this a long time ago. Explore the pain, the weakness. Search for the cause. Find the cure, find the curiosity and do the remedy do the practice."

So, how do we walk in these worlds of our devices, cities, and comfort and at the same time maintain our connection to the wild, the wilderness, and the natural world? It's easy for all of us to overemphasize a dichotomy or disconnect between these aspects of our lives. I find my students and I do that all the time. But perhaps that's not very realistic. "It's all natural, Nate. Cellphones are just another tool, maybe more like a weapon, like a gun. You wouldn't give a baby a gun, so don't give a baby a cellphone."

"Develop a walk of attention, step of acceptance, and a stride of being aware. Walk and move with awareness. Explore your sense of touch, your habit of shoes, your habit of machines, of electronics. Explore the sense of touch of your body by going barefoot. If you feel cold and pain, that is curiosity waking up. [Ask yourself:] What are my reflexes? What are my innate primal reflexes? Reflections? Our muscles and connective tissues are one unit, and they are the biggest sense organ in our body."

Mick showed up at our house not that long ago with some surprising news that he had shared in bits and pieces through email and cryptic text messages. He was setting up his own dojo and training hall with money he had saved over many, many years. This new place is in an undisclosed location in Northern California. This was the culmination and realization of a boyhood dream of his. On a small farm not far from Mount Shasta, Mick continues to train, discover, and ask questions. He continues to use sticks, hammers, and stones, but also plays with cold-water immersion and hot training with kettle bells and other weights in his barn. I can't wait to go and train in this modern day Valhalla, and I hope to bring my children there to play and explore with their wild, primal Uncle Mick.

◆

Having an extended family member so steeped in this path in my life is an inspiration for me and my children. Of course, having my life partner, beloved, and wife, Karen, steeped in this same approach is pretty damn awesome, too.

I've followed and practiced many movement disciplines for decades. Moving like an animal through the forest or mountains is one of my favorite practices, and one I love sharing with others. In my teaching style and personal practice, I'm disciplined, focused, and diligent. But I've learned over the years that I actually take myself, my training, and my teaching a little too seriously. While people crave learning, change, and transformation, and even physical fitness, it doesn't have to be overly focused and serious all the time. In fact, most people who I've trained and seen practice these types of movement actually crave playfulness, creativity, and even silliness. Thank goodness for Karen.

Karen is an embodiment of her middle name—Joy—and is a master at helping people become more playful, spontaneous, and alive. She's been sharing Earthgym with people of all walks of life for over a decade in Seattle, as well as in the wild mountains and forests nearby. In fact, many of our first encounters were platonic Earthgym playdates where we swapped fun, exciting, playful ways of traveling through forest, over boulders on mountainsides, and swinging through trees.

Many of Karen's classes take place at the Greenlake dojo, a select area of Greenlake Park, an amazing urban oasis of water, trees, hills, and wild animals in north central Seattle. When I've gone to Karen's classes, it was not uncommon for me and the other participants to spend time doing push-ups with trees; transforming into wild animals; playing follow the leader games over and around rocks, trees, or even into the water of the lake; and having to spontaneously create our own new exercises with sticks, rocks, and ropes, which were then shared with the group. Smiles, laughter, lightness, and joy abounded.

The Greenlake Dojo Earthgym classes ran for a decade, year-round. This means that for almost 6 months of the year people were practicing this form of exercise in the dark and quite wet winters of the Pacific Northwest. There weren't a lot of other people in the park at those times, allowing Earthgym participants to explore all the nooks and crannies of the park and spend time twirling rocks and hanging upside down from trees without too much scrutiny. Occasionally, they were blessed with a full moon rising over the lake to illuminate their wild and free bodies playing in the winter darkness.

Hiding and playing in the shadows is fun for everyone, but sometimes having an audience is actually a boon for everybody. As Karen describes it, "People get a glimpse of a group of adults running across the trail into the trees, each with a stick in their hand, or hanging upside down from the old cherry tree, or moving with stones on the lake dock as the moon rises over the Cascade Mountains. People see this, smile, become curious, ask questions, and occasionally join in our class, and it opens a doorway of possibility for themselves."

Earthgym helped me discover new ways of moving, playing, and being alive in the outdoors beyond what I already knew and practiced. It was definitely humbling and enlivening to discover a whole new way of relating to movement and the natural world after having taught natural animal movement for over 15 years. It was fun to bring my daughter, Katie, to Karen's classes and run barefoot, hang from trees with ropes while jumping around pretending we were fairies, and then do two-person push-and-pull stick exercises with everybody around us doing the same.

So, why is play so important? What role does it play in our modern world and especially for adults?

Karen and I have both seen that adults often think that play is only for kids. This belief can lead to being really uptight or stressed, being overwhelmed by work and responsibility, and even depression and fatigue. When I was an Anake instructor at WAS, I always worried on the days when we had a lot of games on the agenda. I assumed that people wanted serious training and focus and skills. Instead, game days were hugely popular, and over the years we incorporated more play and games into the curriculum, not less.

Karen puts it nicely: "When the body and mind relax through play, particularly outdoor play, one's mind is not so busy thinking. A different internal process is triggered—one that is more like a child's inner wonder that leads children in immense learning and growth in their early years."

We miss this sense of wonder, play, exploration, and relaxation in today's society; believe it or not, it's an inherent part of hunter-gatherer culture and lifestyles. Exploring and wandering are core routines of finding food and resources, and play and relaxation are a core part of how adults teach children in hunter-gatherer societies. In fact, Jon Young, the founder of WAS, often spoke about how, in the Bushmen culture, adults actually play games or activities first while the children watch. Children have to sit and observe, and then the adults walk away, allowing the kids a free-for-all on game play. Also, in the evening the whole village comes together for a game with a small ball that requires considerable hand-eye coordination and athletic prowess. Adults are "required" to play as much as the kids.

In Earthgym classes, people often showed up frazzled from work, uncomfortable in their bodies, and generally somewhat grumpy. However, they quickly changed after kicking off their shoes, running around barefoot, climbing trees, and playing with sticks, rocks, and ropes. Over time, there were big changes in people who kept attending the classes. Mental health professionals have determined that play for adults can relieve stress by triggering endorphins, improving brain function, stimulating the mind and creativity, and keeping us feeling young and energetic.

"Doing this transformation week after week, year after year builds a resiliency, well-being, and exuberance in people. I've also seen how the joy of our classes become contagious and seep into the people around us," shared Karen.

Long-term students became more malleable and creative. The training unlocked parts of their brain that allowed for more curiosity, creativity, and an extreme version of "thinking outside the box." Recent research has shown that there is an inherent connection between the complexity of our thinking and the complexity of our movement. Neuroplasticity, or our ability to have new neural pathways develop in our brain, is enhanced by complex movement and moving in new ways outside of our normal range. Medical researchers who have shown that seniors who used dance as a form of movement exercise as opposed to conventional fitness training (with lots of repetitious movements) showed a greater degree of neuroplasticity and the ability to push off cognitive decline. This gives new credence to the old saying, "Move it or lose it." This is not just the case for the elderly either. Over 400 studies in neuroscience have now shown the inter-relationship between dance (complicated, rhythmic, multidimensional movement), learning, neuroplasticity, and brain development for people of all ages.

People who are stuck in offices or spend most of their time in front of screens might not even raise their arms above their head all day, or perhaps have only been on perfectly flat surfaces for hours and hours. Imagine what happens when they kick off their shoes and their feet suddenly have thousands of once-dormant nerve endings engaged? Now add in climbing a tree, moving their arms and legs in a far more complicated movement than they've done all day, and suddenly their eyes are engaging with the diverse, complicated three-dimensional, 360-degree beauty of the canopy of a tree. I would venture that they are now able to think and experience reality in ways that they weren't able to at the end of their work day.

Many people relate to the outdoors and nature as a place for recreation and exercise, and, on some level, this is a great place to start. Exercising outside creates health and vitality, and also reduces stress. But just turning the outdoors into another form of being at the gym misses something deeper that happens when we engage with nature. We aren't just supposed to move *through* the natural world as fast as possible hiking or running in heavy shoes or boots that dull our connection to the complexity of the earth beneath our feet. The landscape calls out for us to unlock thousands of years of primal movement and connection with the world around us.

While backpacking and hiking and the joy of exploring a new landscape is important, it's also important to get off trail. It's there that you can truly play, explore, and interact with the landscape in a different way than just in a predetermined pattern. Karen shared several stories of going on "barefoot running quests" under the guidance of Mick, deep in the Hoh rainforest.

"We stopped to climb giant trees, played in the furry moss, laid down on mossy logs, sat still with the streaming sunlight rays dancing on the waving sword ferns, and dunked in the cold fresh waters of the Hoh River. I was transformed and each cell of my body was full of the awe, wonder, and teachings of the Hoh."

The diversity of the experience and the ability to play and have fun with the landscape in no particular way was what really made the experience magical. Unstructured, playful time in nature awakens that connection to our hunter-gatherer roots. In fact, that was what most of our time was at one point as humans. Yes, there was a need to hunt and gather food and resources, but it was a surprisingly small amount of time. A lot of our time historically was spent exploring, wandering, and discovering outside in a rich bio-diverse environment, something that is sorely lacking for many of us within the modern context.

Karen takes this to the next level as one of her core practices: Wonder Wanders. Both for herself and for her students, she builds in time to be aimless, free, and to explore playfully in a landscape. She calls this "hunting for enchantment" and encourages everyone to find time to wander free and easy over the landscape discovering our magic and reawakening a childlike sense of wonder.

What happens when we do this?

"Following our sense of wonder is much more of an intuitive practice, engaging our right brains and sense of inner trust and listening to the landscape, to the earth. These are all things that are no longer that easy for many people to do in our busy, left-brained, always-trying-to-be-productive lives. Yet, this practice opens us to something much greater than our mind chatter and daily stresses. It is a way to find missing qualities such as clarity, insight, inspiration, guidance, rejuvenation, joy, wisdom, and love."

I see this in Karen all the time, and I see what happens when she doesn't get a chance to do these things as a core part of her routine. I track and watch the same tendencies in myself. Building in time in nature to explore, be like an animal, and get off the beaten path makes us happier, healthier, and more creative.

The Origins of Natural Movement

It's hard to say exactly how, when, and where Natural Movement as a form of exercise started. Perhaps the "movement" had never really died out. There are also a bewildering number of movement practices and exercise systems that relate to what I'm covering in this chapter. One place to start is the work of pioneering physical educator Georges Hébert. In the 1900s, Hébert developed a system and philosophy of exercise after watching children play and seeing them regularly effortlessly perform athletic feats that adults could no longer do. His work created the first obstacle course in the world and later heavily influenced the development of parkour.

Parkour grew out of Hébert's philosophy in the 1980s in France, and soon took the obstacle course philosophy to a whole other level by practicing vaults, running, jumping, and falling in highly urbanized settings and producing some truly daring and death-defying feats. Parkour grew rapidly in popularity in the United States and other parts of the world in the late 90s and early 2000s.

Later, Erwan Le Corre developed his system also influenced by Hébert called MovNat, a series of gymnastic-like training and movement exercises that focuses on core human movements: walking, running, crawling, jumping, climbing, lifting, and swimming. MovNat now has instructors around the world. Katie Bowman is one of the main female teachers and leaders in the movement, and she has written a series of books including *Move Your DNA*. Her work revolves around undoing the effects of civilization and a sedentary lifestyle on our bodies.

Other prominent Natural Movement teachers and leaders include Professor Alvaro Romano, who created Ginastica Natural (a form of natural movement combined with Jiu Jitsu training); Ido Portal, who trained UFC fighter and world champion Conor McGregor; and Scott Sonnon, who has created several systems, including Circular Strength Training and TacFit, which combine natural movement, mobility, and various training tools to bring elite fitness training to Special Forces groups and others.

Finally, if you are interested in more specific information about the benefits of spending time barefoot and some interesting science behind the benefits, check out the book *Earthing*.

The kinds of movement I'm describing here in this chapter easily blend, melt, and flow into other mainstream disciplines, such as yoga, CrossFit, and even martial arts. For years, I've danced back and forth between teaching animal forms, studying internal martial arts, and mixing in whatever other movement discipline I've been exposed to. The results have really helped me out, allowing me to retain a vitality, flexibility, and liveliness in my 40s. However, I'm not the only one who has been doing this kind of experimentation.

Last winter, I was able to reconnect with an old friend, Ben Sanford, the founder and main teacher for Primal Edge Tribal

Arts, a survival school on the Olympic Peninsula. At his school, Ben combines survival skills, movement, martial arts, fitness, and personal coaching for optimal wellness and transformation. For years, Ben had been sending his students to WAS for specific kinds of training, and I had been trying to figure out a way to bring him to WAS for our students as well. On a very cold, wet February weekend I succeeded, and only a few hours into the program I could see Ben's gifts and skills unleashed in our students. He led a two-person stick-fighting play and exploration workshop in the woods and, within 20 minutes, everybody was alive, excited, and clanging away with sticks, despite the deep, cold rain.

Ben has had the nickname "Tarzan" for years due to his incredibly strong, beefy physique and his love of playing and climbing in trees and getting others to do the same. Ben sees tree climbing as analogous to rock climbing, only trees are way more dynamic. Per Ben, "They move. It's like climbing a moving, living, rock climbing feature." The epitome of tree climbing is tree travel, which is moving from tree to tree over a large distance without touching the ground.

I am familiar with this technique. One of my favorite challenges for my students was to have them climb from vine maple to vine maple for over a hundred yards without touching the ground. The act of working against gravity and needing to have four points of contact at all times reveals a playful dance through a mossy wonderland of verdant green tree trunks above the ground. Ben is a master of such play and stunts and shared a story of when he traveled downslope at Yosemite National Park through young oak trees. Ben was able to beat out his cousin in a race, who was running on the ground downhill through a thousand feet of elevation drop.

Ben's love of trees and tree climbing began as a child as he grew up on the Olympic Peninsula. Like so many kids of my generation, Ben was gifted with a childhood of unstructured after school time and free weekends—a rarity in our modern world consumed with over-structuring of children's free time with activities. We shared stories of being wild boys, being barefoot and bare-chested constantly playing and challenging our friends and peers in our packs to climb higher, jump farther, and reach more through all sorts of natural obstacles. This natural play became more serious and sophisticated when Ben discovered the Tarzan books of Edgar Rice Burroughs when he was 14. He also discovered Tom Brown Jr.'s books at the same time, and he compensated for the lack of mentors in his real life by allowing these archetypal heroes to come alive through stories.

This wild childhood, as well as deeper studies through his teen and adult years, has led Ben to work with students of all walks of life to find their gifts and awaken their own inner heroic nature.

So, for a man who embodies the very spirit of the natural movement in both his work and his everyday life, the answer to the question of why natural movement is so important came easily to him:

"We are nature. The more we can experience direct contact with the wild world, the more we can know ourselves. We have been moving [with a purpose] in nature for hundreds of thousands of years and have co-evolved with the world as a moving organism."

Exactly.

Here's a term Ben introduced to me: the cowardly caveman fallacy. What is it? This is the notion that our ancestors suffered greatly huddling in caves, in constant stress and fear over food and predators. There seems to be a pervasive cultural story that if we don't have all of our creature comforts of modern society we will suffer greatly. Research is beginning to show that the opposite might actually be true. Our modern human life is filled with false stressors alarming and overwhelming our nervous systems, and studies of contemporary hunter-gatherers show that they work way less than we do and spend a huge amount of time in relative relaxation.

Ben summed up this attitude and understanding nicely. "We need to go from Man vs. Wild to Man is Wild and remember our archetypal primal self."

Almost all the classes Ben teaches go outside, and, just like Mick and Karen, one of his goals is to get people out of their shoes and barefoot. The transformations and impacts of going barefoot are fast and profound, and they help us with the challenges of our sedentary lifestyles. But, of course, change can be challenging to start.

"As we seek comfortable, protected, and easy lifestyles, we are changing the course of our evolution . . . wearing thick shoes or heavy protective clothing, we end up with a 'proprioceptive lag,' or sensory distortion, which leads to numerous problems," Ben explains. "Our behaviors become incongruent with our reality. With distorted senses, we misinterpret the honest feedback that the laws of nature give to us through the simple sensations, feelings, and instincts that we fail to notice."

But this can change quickly for people. Ben has seen it in his own students. By practicing stalking games where people sneak up on each other, paint their face with natural camouflage, and go barefoot, the students began moving completely differently and, perhaps more importantly, their entire being and awareness shifted too.

This brings up another important point. In my many years of teaching animal movement, while the animal embodiment aspect of the movements is certainly important, students really come alive and "get it" when they start playing games stalking each other and trying to sneak up on one another without being seen. Ben agrees.

"As fun as tree climbing and all kinds of gymnastic parkour-like, flow-producing movements can be, I think stalking may be one of the finest expressions of human movement because of its fusion with nature. It's a useful human movement we've been doing forever. Stalking revolves around safety or staying alive and finding food.

That'll stick around! When people tap into it, it activates a different world. It puts you in a flow state/fusion activity with self and world, all the layers."

I agree. It's stunning to see how quickly kids, adults, elders, and people of all ages sink into stalking and sneaking as a fundamental human movement. Instantly, they are present; gone are the distractions of video games or the office. When we do this, we step into a deeper level of primal awareness and movement. This is the kind of movement that allowed our ancestors to hunt food or, even more importantly, avoid being eaten. Tapping into this is very powerful. In fact, you could run a whole immersion week or two just off this principle.

Which is actually what Ben does some of the time as he teaches the martial arts portion of Tom Brown Jr.'s Scout class and runs his Scout Protector class. During these classes and this kind of training, one of the things that's emphasized is learning to make contact with the ground and the world without making a sudden lurching commitment. As Ben says, "We are not living a controlled fall." In fact, we are learning to move with a landscape, not through a landscape, and stalking and sneaking become a slow, elegant Tai Chi dance of person and land fusing together. I've seen people lose a sense of self and enter deep states of awareness. They actually, "Lose their mind and become their senses." (This is a common saying of Dan Millman, author of *Way of the Peaceful Warrior*.) I relish the times I slip into this state and find a deep peace inside. An internal longing I didn't even know I had becomes fulfilled through this graceful fusion of self and environment. The primal inner and outer quietness of our ancient ancestors comes alive.

Talking and sharing with Ben provoked my own many memories of stalking and sneaking with students. I remembered times in Hawaii hanging out in a strawberry guava tree as adult students walked right below me, or hiding right behind a gecko climbing on a wild ginger flower. The students were so focused on the gecko that they couldn't see me standing right behind it. Hawaii was just one of many landscapes and places where I got to feel this particular thrill. I was lucky enough to have sunk into this world of stalking, sneaking, and camouflage in the deep mossy forest of the Pacific Northwest, the dry harsh landscape of the Sonoran Desert, the oak highlands of Northern California, and the Rocky Mountains of Idaho and Montana. Some of my most magical primal moments have happened when sinking into this stillness and awareness.

But one place sticks out above all, as the site where so many rich experiences and memories sit of engaging this merging of landscape, inner silence, and invisible movement: the snowberry, arrow-leafed balsam root, and ponderosa pine hillsides of central Washington. This was the location of Scout Camp (week one of The Gauntlet) and the culmination of movement and awareness training at Anake.

It's important to note that there are a lot of students who don't take right away to crawling through the bushes like an animal or climbing trees or twirling heavy rocks over their heads. We all have different levels of comforts and discomforts, different proclivities, talents, and skills. Clearly, moving like an animal unencumbered, free, and wild through a diverse landscape is one of the things I love. And, while not all of the students I've taught over the years have taken an immediate liking to this wild, primal form of exercise, almost everybody has during the culmination of that training.

Enveloping yourself in the world of secrecy, stealth, and full-time awareness training in small groups that makes up Scout Camp quickly makes clear the practical application of animal forms, barefoot, and natural movement training. When you're moving day and night in a small team through an unfamiliar landscape, trying to not be seen as you sneak up on other groups, moving like a wild animal becomes damn useful.

Even for the students who didn't like or understand animal forms, Scout Camp serves to awaken their inner primal awareness.

Participants shared reflections of having truly powerful break-through moments of feeling like an animal for extended periods of time, or of having their thinking/talking mind go quiet in a way that they had never really experienced but had only heard about in stories of people who practice meditation for years and years. These people discovered their primal mind and body—both alive and awakened—as their souls merged with the land around them.

Seeing, watching, and feeling the palpable change in people is a satisfying and soul-nourishing experience. Seeing wild and free humans come fully alive with a sparkle in their eyes and an electricity pulsing through their bodies was what sustained me and my fellow instructors in this work for many years. It's another part of the primal journey, just like fire-making, stone tools, or learning to gather wild food.

I am reminded of something a very wise elder once shared. Gilbert Walking Bull was a Lakota elder, healer, and medicine person who came and taught at Wilderness Awareness School for some time. His teachings and presence were enormous, powerful, and very influential for many students. One of the core teachings he shared involved what happens to people when they spend lots of time getting really connected to nature. He described sacred and totally natural qualities that would emerge in people, our birthright as humans.

One of these qualities was called *Wozani*, a Lakota word that is complex to translate but loosely refers to the vitality of a wild animal, a kind of wild electricity that moves through you. Watching the change in people from doing wild, natural movement, seeing what happens to people from attending Scout Camp, seeing the changes that happen in Karen's students after playing at Earthgym classes, or seeing what happens to people when they remember the joy of climbing trees, I can understand what Gilbert was getting at. It all starts by simply taking off our shoes, feeling the ground with our unencumbered human bare feet, and letting ourselves play wild and free.

CHAPTER 4

The Paleo Revolution: Making Our Food and Lives Wild Again

We must first understand that all things that live on the earth must eat. . . . It is how we take these things that makes the difference, that makes us caretakers and not a disease. We must take things first with great thanksgiving and appreciation in our heart. . . . We must take that life in a sacred manner, in a way that will benefit the land rather than destroy it.

—Coyote Thunder, apache elder,
quoted in *Grandfather* by Tom Brown Jr.

The smell of blood from a deer carcass is unmistakable. It is pungent, slightly sweet, and unbelievably musky. The smell was all over me as my arms were coated up to my elbows in sticky deer blood. If this was some pseudo-reality show for television, then it would be a deer that I had hunted with a bow and arrow that I had created myself. And, while I've made my own bows and arrows before, this deer came from a much more modern context: it was fresh roadkill.

Processing a fresh deer carcass was one of the most intense experiences of my life. Many people have this happen when they first help butcher a large animal. It completely changes their relationship to food, to meat, to life and death. Life and death, blood and guts, food and meat . . . it doesn't get much more primal than this. For me, the first experience came when I was in my early 30s. My friend and fellow instructor, Johnny Miller, had brought the deer to a staff training day. Johnny's "present" was a big surprise and a big hit. He had found the deer on the road on the way to the school's property that morning, and a few of us spent a good chunk of the day processing it.

Skinning, gutting, and preparing an animal that large takes a lot of human muscle and power, and it's definitely a task that goes quicker and easier with some company. Johnny, Dan Corcoran, Lindsay Huettman, and I took turns taking apart the deer.

Johnny invited me to take care of the deer's lungs. I reached my arm into the buck's chest cavity and, under Johnny's instruction, very carefully cut the deer's trachea and pulled out the lungs. The chest cavity was incredibly warm, almost hot. Sticking my arm in felt like I was sticking it into a living animal. It took a lot of care to not cut myself with the knife or not puncture the chest cavity unnecessarily. I felt dazed and overwhelmed.

A few hours later we sat around a fire we had made with a fire kit. We had cleaned ourselves up some, and Johnny had given us each a freezer bag full of meat for helping. Chunks of venison roasted on sticks over the fire, making us salivate in anticipation. We were sore and tired, but also lit up. After a while, we nibbled on some smoky, succulent chunks. I've never tasted meat that good, and energy from the meat hit me hard. I felt wild, alive, and vital. My sight sharpened, and I noticed details in the forest all around me.

People who give death to an animal, particularly for the first time, come away with similar thoughts and feelings: awe, reverence, sadness, appreciation. Many feel that this is an experience everyone should have, especially if they want to eat meat.

The world of food is changing rapidly around us. A decade or so ago, the Paleo diet sparked a revolution in the way we think about how we eat. People started to challenge the notion of a high-carbohydrate, high-grain diet as being healthy, and now dozens of diets have spun off of the Paleo diet as people have started to think very deeply about the food we eat and how it shapes who we are. What can our ancestors tell us about how to eat healthy or how to be healthy? What can wild foods do for us? Can they help us heal or be healthy and nourish the planet at the same time?

When I think of the importance of wild foods and a wild diet, my mind immediately turns to a place I get to visit often, run by two friends of mine. Hawthorn Farm is the vision of Alexia Allen and her partner, Daniel Kirchhof. One of the last times I was there, I was invited to partake of a soup on the stove.

I sipped a little of the broth of the soup as I made my way into the woods nearby for a men's gathering at their Storytelling Yurt. The broth was from a goat that Daniel and Alexia had raised and then given death to from their 8-acre farm. However, the soup also contained elk meat and a variety of vegetables harvested from the land. This was not a special or atypical meal for Daniel and Alexia. They eat like this all the time.

In fact, their courtship and their life revolved around food with a degree of intimacy and connection that is rarely experienced in modern 21st century America—a connection that was pretty much the norm for all of us for most of human history. In addition to running Hawthorn Farm, Alexia and Daniel have both been survival skills instructors for years. Alexia and I were Anake instructors together for 3 years, and Daniel had been a youth and adult instructor at Twin Eagles School in Idaho for over a decade before meeting Alexia and moving to Hawthorn Farm. Hawthorn Farm now serves as a community gathering space that teaches traditional skills and crafts, such as butchering chickens, archery, bow-making, and spinning wool. Alexia and Daniel fell in love through their relationship with food, food that was wild and harvested by themselves or people they knew.

After ending a previous relationship, Alexia had this continued visceral image of a male hunter bringing her elk meat in a tepee. While sad over the thought that this image might not become her reality, Alexia busied herself running her small-scale homestead farm and wrapping up her tenure at Wilderness Awareness School. But it was not too long after Alexia's vision of longing that Daniel came into her life, and—believe it or not—he was an elk hunter who had just spent a stretch of time living in a tepee.

Daniel grew up hunting elk and deer, fishing, and gathering huckleberries in rural Montana. His food journey did a complete 360, first turning completely away from meat, and then leaving his vegan diet for what he saw as an ethical connection that was possible with wild meat. Daniel reminisced about a night sharing antelope steaks over a fire with friends during a snowy Montana night. The food felt like pure medicine to Daniel, and since that time he hasn't eaten meat that he doesn't have some connection to (either raising it, hunting it, or being given it by someone else doing the same).

Daniel and Alexia's first date included Daniel bringing elk from over the mountains to Alexia's farm homestead, and the two of them took on the first of many "food challenges." This was an idea inspired by one of Daniel's students who had spent two weeks living only off of food he harvested himself. Daniel and Alexia spent that first food challenge harvesting food off the farm to combine with what Daniel brought. And wild food, hand-harvested food, or food grown and harvested on their farm have been a core of their life together ever since.

Alexia and Daniel don't mince words around food, modernity, and what is happening for so many of us as we have lost our primal connection with food.

"The aisles of a grocery store are a bit like prostitution—a quick transaction of calories for cash without the need for a loving relationship. Hidden stories of abused and neglected landscapes lie behind brightly colored boxes and cellophane packages," said Alexia when describing why they do what they do.

I've seen students come to a similar realization over time when they experience the wonder of eating steamed nettles for the first time or the exhilaration and playful joy of cramming your face full of wild huckleberries. When they notice how they feel when they eat wild foods, there is a dawning realization of a connection so fundamental and pure. And yet, simultaneously, there is a deep sadness around what is available at the common grocery store or served at the restaurants nearby. One of Alexia's deepest realizations from eating from her farm and doing many wild foods trips is that she is literally made out of what she eats, and her health is directly connected to the health of the soil on her farm.

But Alexia and Daniel don't just hang out on their farm and do their powerful local, subversive work in the suburbs of Seattle. Every year they go on a walkabout, traveling with minimal gear and living off the land as much as they can for at least a week. Why?

"We love transforming suburbia, but we need to get out of our safe, agricultural ruts every year and remember the beauty of the wilder, more original world!" summarized Alexia.

Alexia and Daniel's trips are truly epic, and they have a ton of wild stories of what has happened, what has worked, and what has been a true challenge when going on their walkabouts.

On their very first walkabout they journeyed to an old-growth cedar forest where there was a plethora of huckleberries. Daniel and Alexia were so inspired by the richness of the ecology of the old-growth forest that they now use that as a model for the 5-acre patch of woods on their property. Their forest stewardship plan has a vision of the land returned to old-growth cedar.

When I've gone on my own walkabouts, the quick calories from consuming wild berries have been a lifesaver. I've learned to time my wild wanders for when some wild food is fully abundant. Having a plentiful supply of berries around makes the work of building shelter, making fire, and finding safe water all that much easier. But this modern insight and timing of matching one's rhythms to when a specific wild food is prolific is not new at all. It's actually how ancestral food harvesting was accomplished, and you can easily and predictably trace seasonal human migration routes in response to food resources waxing and waning. Many tribal groups throughout history have had both a summer and winter core area that differ in what foods are available in each location.

Alexia and Daniel have learned some variation on this lesson time and time again on their wild food journeys. They once sheltered above 6,000 feet amid ice and snow while having to work hard all day to harvest handfuls of lily bulbs for food. Every evening they gave each other handfuls of calorie-rich bulbs they had gathered from the day. The combination of these precious handfuls of lily bulbs with so many mountain huckleberries kept them alive in below freezing temperatures at night.

It can be difficult to find sufficient fat and protein while doing a survival walkabout. While finding wild greens and wild berries can be somewhat easy, especially seasonally, finding a source of wild nuts or hunting and killing your own meat is much harder and rarer. Frog legs from a bullfrog you caught by hand or a tiny, wriggly, slimy trout you chased to the bank and managed to grasp suddenly seem like a true luxury and feast.

Daniel and Alexia learned this lesson on one of their other trips. They discovered an unusual richness of wild pine nuts that they were able to pry from roasted white-barked pinecones. The cache of pine nuts gave them a steady supply of fat and protein to mix with gooseberries and currants to produce a much more primal and wild form of what we all know as trail mix.

But why do Daniel and Alexia feel a need to do this, especially when they have such an amazing farm that they live on and tend so intimately and fully?

"Eating wild foods keeps us in touch with the world beyond our farm," they shared. "It connects us to the long history our ancestors had before entering into domesticated relationships with our common food plants and animals. Hunting and gathering awaken something primal, original, and wildly alive in our bodies and in our attitudes. Not only that, these original natives of this continent, like elk, deer, salmon, huckleberry, wild rose, kelp, and others, are perfectly attuned to their landscapes and are always perfectly in season and usually more nutritionally dense than their domestic counterparts."

Even if we return to the simple rhythms of farm life, that ancestral, hunter-gatherer instinct is wild, alive, and vital.

Over time, Daniel and Alexia grew concerned about the impact they were having on wild places. This was not out of neglect or lack of awareness. They had always selected places that were truly abundant in whatever resources they were harvesting. But even after visiting a place one time, they realized that many of the food resources they were relying on were rapidly disappearing due to climate change. The white-barked pine, which had provided their delicious and nutrient-rich pine nut staple, was dying out in vast numbers and not being replaced quickly. Daniel and Alexia chose to start bringing their own wild foods they had harvested throughout the year on their trips instead of relying solely on the resources of the place they were going to.

As Daniel put it, "In the wild places, living as simply as our ancestors we come to terms with our own far-reaching impacts and interventions on this planet. Even on a trip with no knife and no fire, we still step on plants and eat berries."

Now for their trips, Alexia and Daniel spend the whole year getting ready. I've found that this is a useful method, as well. Many people expect survival instructors to walk into the woods naked all the time and simply harvest everything they need effortlessly in a day or two. This myth does not meet the reality of practicing survival, and choosing to bring certain things with you on your walkabout can make the experience way more successful and fulfilling. For Daniel and Alexia, that might mean hiking in with a haunch of elk meat they harvest off the road. For me, it might mean bringing wild pemmican I've made with venison jerky, dried salal, and rendered bear fat.

Alexia takes this wild food challenge into her everyday life and doesn't hesitate to throw a roadkill squirrel in the freezer for a wild food trip down the road. Who knows when you'll need some dried squirrel haunch for a trip?

While Daniel and Alexia's wild foods walkabouts are a testament to their skill, knowledge, and connection to nature, they have also accomplished a goal so far beyond these walkabouts, one that sets a high bar for people and their relationship with food in 21st-century America. During 2017, Alexia and Daniel ate nothing for a whole year except food that they gathered, grew, harvested, or hunted themselves or was given to them by someone else doing the same thing. No grocery stores, no restaurants, no Amazon Fresh, no big agriculture—nothing that wasn't raised by hand. This daunting and incredible feat was in many ways the ultimate survival challenge and test of self-reliance. During this time, Daniel and Alexia took on challenges, such as dehydrating seawater to produce their own salt and harvesting wild seaweed so they wouldn't become deficient in iodine. They also received wonderful gifts from friends and former students who wanted to support them on this journey. The gifts included acorn mush from the East Coast and wild bog cranberries covered in big leaf maple syrup—quite the treats when you've been relying on squash, potatoes, chicken eggs, and kale as your main staples for months!

I asked Alexia and Daniel what they've learned and taken away from these wild food walkabouts and their 1-year food challenge. As you can imagine, it can be tough to summarize such huge experiences. Heck, for me just spending a few days living off blackberries and hazelnuts tends to completely alter my reality for quite a while. But they did have important insights to share.

For Alexia, it was about realizing how important the health of the soil of her farm is: "I'm made out of what I eat. And oh, right . . . that's true for everybody. There's a reason why food traditions are the way they are. Dried clams were transported and traded to the interior for a reason: iodine deficiency. The minerals in the soil are different in different places. People have to manage land in different ways, and I want to grow nutrient-dense food here."

For Daniel, it was a realization about how divorced we've become from our relationship with food: "People say, 'I'm working to put food on the table,' which is sort of true, but not really. They haven't actually done anything that directly with that food to put it on the table. It's so complex right now with government and corporations, we forget how simple life is and can be. Taking a break from that and trying to live in simple clothes and eat food that is hand-harvested. At its core, life is pretty simple: feed ourselves and each other, walk around, breathe. Get along and share love and stay warm enough. That's all we have to do. We might be happier, healthier, and less stressed if we do just that."

For the two of them, it's hard to know what the future holds for their way of life. We all expressed concerns about the ecological impacts and collapses we have seen in our own lifetimes, both in wild places and nearby. Perhaps, there is a setting sun on the wild food trips Alexia and Daniel have undertaken, but they are both committed to something more hopeful for the future generations.

"I want the future generations to see orcas jump out of the water instead of more skyscrapers. Let's sink into wild foods and primal ways to remind ourselves we don't need much. This can help us remember the limitations of the planet we live on," said Daniel.

It's not possible or practical for all of us to suddenly return to a full-on hunter-gatherer lifestyle. With our current population, we would devastate the wild food resources rapidly. But that doesn't mean we can't have those ways of life and understanding inform the choices we do make.

"I want to keep moving to the horizon of the hunter-gatherer. For me, that is my ethical horizon. My favorite way of being with the world is a Stone Age context, even if just for limited periods of time," shared Alexia.

I agree completely. It's a way of keeping our primal journey alive in the 21st century.

Rewilding Our Food and Diet

Going back perhaps as far as the 1800s, there has been debate about our modern diet versus the way ancient people ate. There has been a consistent and persistent argument that our modern civilized food is not healthy for us and is slowly killing us in some way. The usual culprit for this malaise is grains, and there is very interesting and compelling evidence that grains and other high-carbohydrate foods can be highly problematic when consumed in excess. There is at the very least strong anecdotal evidence that high-carbohydrate foods and refined sugar are linked to many "modern" conditions that were quite rare or completely absent in ancient cultures, including Type II diabetes, obesity, dental cavities and abnormalities, heart disease, and various forms of cancer.

Weston Price was one of the first in modern times to advocate for a high-protein, high animal product–based diet with a minimum of grains. His work was based on well-documented anthropological research showing the impact of introducing grains to hunter-gatherer cultures within one generation. In his research, dramatic photos show complete changes in jaw structure and teeth in the human species within one generation of introducing refined grains and modern foods.

The term *Paleolithic Diet*, or simply *Paleo*, took off in the late 2000s and the 2010s as Loren Cordain published the immensely popular *The Paleo Diet*. Cordain is a professor of Exercise and Health Physiology at Colorado State University, and while there has been both popular and professional criticism of his theories and ideas, there are equally valid arguments supporting the notion that our hunter-gatherer ancestors were considerably healthier than we are now. In fact, there's pretty clear evidence that our health declined significantly after we started eating grains. Cordain and two MD colleagues of his wrote a paper entitled,

"Evolutionary Health Promotion: A Consideration of Common Counterarguments" for the professional health journal *Preventive Medicine*. By 2012–13, "Paleo Diet" was by far the most popular Google search term related to food, nutrition, and diet.

Around the same time as Cordain's work was taking off and becoming popular, professional triathlete and marathoner Mark Sisson began writing his immensely popular *Mark's Daily Apple* blog that advocated for what he called "Primal Eating and Lifestyle." Mark ended up publishing *The Primal Blueprint* and several follow-up books that advocated not just for changing how we eat, but also adopting the lifestyle habits of hunter-gatherer people to lead healthier lives. This included how we sleep, play, rest, and exercise in emulation of what we think our ancestors did.

For those interested in Stone Age–level hunting and hunting with their own bows and arrows, Bill McConnell is the best I know at this skill. Bill was an instructor for Tom Brown Jr. at the Tracker School, and he has successfully hunted his own food for over 2 decades with bows and arrows he's made himself out of all-natural materials, including stone arrowheads he flintknapped on his arrows. Bill has a program that teaches these kinds of skills located in Montana called Past Skills.

The hunting side of the hunter-gatherer lifestyle is pretty intriguing and exciting for most people. It seems to be way sexier than the whole gathering piece. But the reality is that, in most places, the gathering and eating of plant foods was at least as important, and probably way more important, than the hunting of animals. Except in very extreme environments, such as the arctic or very high in the mountains, plants made up the core of what we ate, and they are the base of the food chain of our very existence. Not only that, plants also served as the basic form of our medicine for tens of thousands of years. Every known hunter-gatherer tribe ever studied has an extensive pharmacopeia of plants that they use to treat medical conditions, and humans are not alone in this. Scientists have recently realized that chimps, elephants, and bears also use medicinal plants to heal themselves when they are sick.

Plants are such an important part of what it means to be human that our eyes are actually specifically adapted for them. *We actually see more shades of green than any other color.* It's speculated that this is to help us distinguish subtle differences in plant species. In fact, green is such an important part of our lives that medical researchers have figured out that if we paint classrooms or hospital rooms a light shade of green then people will calm down significantly. It's almost as if we have a biological expectation to be surrounded by green living things . . . actually it's exactly that we have a biological expectation to be surrounded by green living things!

This relationship with plants and with plants as food informs almost every story in this book. It's no mistake that both Tom Elpel and Tamarack Song mention early memories of gathering wild plants for food with family members. One of my earliest memories is also of gathering wild asparagus with my father by the railroad tracks not too far from our house. These are examples of some of the original memories we as a human species have had for millennia.

For over a decade, I was lucky enough to teach wild plants as food and medicine at the Anake program. I was joined in this endeavor by Lindsay Huettman, an ethnobotanist with years of training in multiple bioregions regarding people and plants. She has designed her own plant apprenticeship for people who want to go deep with her for a year to study plants as food, medicine, craft, and clothing. We have joked over the years about our varying levels of plant dorkiness, and sometimes when we taught together it seemed as if we had a subtle competition going on about who was more passionate and excited about plants.

The two of us joined other instructors on a fall wild harvest day where we gathered as many different kinds of food plants as we could in one day. This was followed up by spending a day processing, drying, and transforming all that food at Hawthorn Farm with Daniel and Alexia. Later in the year, we co-taught a plant class where students could learn to make tinctures, teas, and salves out of local plants. Then we finished off the year with a spring wild edibles class, having students chomping on dandelion fritters, nettle soup, stir-fried cattail, and a wild greens salad to prepare them for their end of the year survival trip.

One of the things we tried to do with these classes is break down the "green wall." This is a phenomenon of people really struggling to differentiate one plant from another and also having huge difficulty with remembering plants. Basically, everything just looks like "green stuff." The green wall is another example of our collective amnesia about ancestral knowledge and skills. In ancestral cultures, breaking down the green wall is one of the first things kids learned to do. This has happened quite naturally in my family. Both of my daughters know dozens of plants. The youngest one, Tara, is only 5.

Lindsay has seen this, too, in her work and also sees an almost paralyzing fear of poisonous plants in her students.

"Most people are really intimidated by the plant world at first and/or have been told that all wild plants are really dangerous. I think this is such a disservice as most of my students are really wanting to learn but are afraid to," she said.

Lindsay's connections with plants also started in her childhood, and the green world was a solace for her when things were tough at home. So many of us have similar stories of finding a tree, patch of forest, a creek or lakeshore, or just our backyard where we went to take a break, get away from conflict, or find relief from challenging home situations. It's almost as if plants and the green world are a natural balm or salve for the wounds we feel at an emotional and soul level.

This is a part of Lindsay's work, as well. She runs Soul Stewards Counseling, doing counseling and grief work with people of all ages. The work of the land, healing emotional wounds, and creating new ways forward are all intertwined in Lindsay's path.

As a grief counselor, Lindsay encourages us to go to the plants to help us in troubled times. "Go to the plants. Go to the cedar trees. Go for a big hug. The forest and wild places are there to hold and help us with our grief. It's all a huge container. But don't forget to give back when you can. It's about reciprocity."

Lindsay's approach to plants, healing, and our connections to land can show up in surprising ways, as well. While one of Lindsay's main passions is plants and ethnobotany, she has also spent stints as a river guide on the Skagit River, as a core instructor at the Anake program, and even a time on a backwoods farm in the upper Skagit harvesting and canning a huge amount of her own food, including wild salmon.

The Wilderness Walkabout, or simply the Walkabout, is a badass 1-week program put on by WAS and is basically a moving, hiking, survival intensive that covers miles and miles (as opposed to a basecamp-style survival experience). In the program, participants take minimal gear (like clothes, a knife, a poncho, and a water bottle) and cover a huge amount of terrain, living off the land as they go. There are plenty of surprises along the way, and participants are pushed to their physical and psychological edge. Lindsay has been an instructor in the program for a decade, and as far as I know is the only female lead instructor in the program to this date.

Annually, Lindsay still instructs at this program even while she has her private practice, her plant apprenticeship, and pursues a PhD in ecopsychology. Even though she is extremely busy, the Walkabout is still vital.

Over the course of those 7 days, it is shocking how much people change. It's amazing how deep people go into themselves every single year while eating dandelions on the go, harvesting nuts, and munching on pine needles. People become vital and alive, engaging with a movable feast, and the experience becomes a true rite of passage for modern people who wish to transform back into their wild, free selves. People go from being uptight, scared, and physically uncomfortable into a more relaxed body language. They are able to remember how to feel joy and pleasure as they become at ease.

For many doing the walkabout there is a big chance to experience new emotional connections with plants, the land, and each other. Our modern-day disconnection from the world around us creates a system of perpetual grief and discord. If we have a deep biological expectation to be emotional—physically, and perhaps spiritually connected to the land, food, plants, and each other—what happens when we don't have that? Disconnection, numbness, sadness, and an emptiness that can cause us to consume almost endlessly trying to fill the void inside.

Fortunately, this disconnection can be healed, and sometimes surprisingly quickly. Lindsay explains it as similar to attachment theory. In this commonly and widely accepted psychological theory, the kind of emotional attachment we have to our parents when we are young greatly influences our social interactions for the rest of our lives. If we don't have a healthy attachment pattern as infants, it can be very tricky to develop successful adult relationships. But what if we not only need healthy attachment patterns to our adult caregivers but also to the plants, birds, animals, and trees of our environment? What happens if we are given the opportunity to repair those attachments as adults? Can we rediscover our primal connection to these aspects of the world around us?

Lindsay shared one story with me of a man who went on the Walkabout who spent most of the program being quite agitated and uncomfortable. He was short and irritable with the instructors and his fellow students, and it seemed he really didn't want to be there. In fact, as they approached a culminating river crossing over halfway through the course, he seemed as if he was going to demand to be evacuated from the remote wilderness setting. Lindsay was instructing the course with Dan Corcoran, and they weren't quite sure what to do. But they had one more trick in their bag . . . or rather one more plant in the bag.

For years, the go-to plant offering for Walkabout participants who were having a hard time was *Artemisia tridenta* or western sagebrush. Just when it seemed like Mr. Grumpy was ready to call for an evac, they handed him some sagebrush to spend some time alone with.

I don't know if he burned some of the sagebrush, rubbed it on his body, or just inhaled some of the crushed leaves with their unbelievably pure, pungent scent, but the man was completely transformed. He finally crossed the river along with everyone else, and then he was not only not grumpy, but he got along terrifically with the rest of the crew. He hugged people, smiling and experiencing joy for the first time in perhaps many years. Needless to say, it was another successful Walkabout and further proof that our ancestral, primal blueprint is not that far below the surface, waiting to get out.

———

"We were Paleo before paleo was a thing. . . ."

This became a common quip among different folks in the survival field as the Paleo diet explosion took off. It's ironic that so many people have embraced such a major dietary shift as the Paleo diet but haven't expanded that to other areas of their life. I'm hoping that stories like those shared here will start to expand for people what being Paleo really means.

After all, leaving grains out of your diet because they are really a relatively "new" food for human beings is a direct action honoring the fact that we are physically still like hunter-gatherers. Even other trendy diets, such as intermittent fasting, are based on the idea that our physiology is used to having booms and busts in our ability to hunt and gather food. And the Keto diet mimics the diets of existing hunter-gatherers, such as the Inuit, who have large amounts of fat in their diet as one of their main sources of calories.

A new diet trend, called the Carnivore diet, demands people only eat large quantities of meat. While this is certainly extreme, it too is a throwback to when our ancestors had a successful hunt.

Can you imagine how much meat you would eat if you were a part of a successful mammoth hunt? You'd probably eat nothing but mammoth meat for days and days.

Regardless of our particular dietary choices, I have seen people transformed by learning to give death to an animal or participate in a "sacred harvest" of an animal or even plant for food. Kids and adults of all ages become totally alive when eating wild berries or harvesting their first set of nettles and realizing they can eat this green "stinging" plant.

Not that long ago I was with a group of students on the Tolt River near my house. There was a massive run of pink salmon happening. This occurs every 4 years, and our focus for that day of class was on harvesting food from the landscape. While we usually focused on plants, we were easily distracted by the massive amount of potential food swimming, fighting, thrashing, and mating in the water nearby.

I had brought along my fishing pole that day, just in case. It was definitely a little strange to explain to students that we couldn't just club the fish or catch them by hand. The fish were so thick and in such vast numbers, we could easily have hand harvested half-a-dozen fish within an hour. Instead, we had to follow the rather obscure and arcane fishing laws on the river. Some of the students wanted to dive in after the fish or carve simple spears and go after the ample aquatic prey nearby. I understood how they felt, and I still don't understand why it's legal for fishing boats and companies to scoop up millions of fish in mile-wide nets, but catching fish in the rivers nearby requires the use of a small lure on the end of a fishing pole. To channel this frustration, I informed everyone that if we caught a fish, we could kill it, cook it, and eat it right there. So together, we followed the fish and looked for suitable spots for me to use my rod and lures.

By some stroke of luck, we succeeded in catching a pink that day by totally modern, legal means. It was definitely a group effort, and it's pretty difficult to convince a fish that isn't interested in eating anymore to bite the lure you flick in front of it. While catching the fish was fun, what happened next was awesome.

We gathered around the fish, and said some words of thanks and praise to the fish, to the river, and to life itself. In the bright autumn sun amid swirling, twirling golden cottonwood leaves falling from the trees, we gave death to the salmon in as sacred a way as we could manage. The students then made an impromptu rock fire pit and proceeded to get a bow-drill fire going in under ten minutes.

Together, we cleaned the salmon with our knives, and then cut it into large chunks. The chunks were placed on hot stones at the edges of the fire, and we took turns turning the fish to cook it evenly. It cooked in a surprisingly short time, and soon we were gleefully stuffing chunks of hot, juicy salmon into our mouth. The juices dribbled on our faces and clothes, and everyone began to giggle and share stories around the fire. Eventually, we ate the whole fish and returned the bones and skin to the river. Bellies full, we hid all traces of our fire and wandered away from that spot.

There was a lightness in our step and liveliness in our actions that hadn't been there before. Perhaps it was simply the fun and joy of the experience. Maybe the vitality and energy of eating meat so fresh it had literally been alive a few minutes before crept into us. Or maybe it was something else, something wild and ancient: the deep satisfaction of participating in the life and death of our food, something that humans have been doing for a very long time.

CHAPTER 5

Deep Nature Connection: Our Longing to Be Like the Bushmen

Each day when I open my eyes and see the sun, I am happy. Even when I think about the poverty and hunger around me, I am still happy. I immediately start the day with manageable things—looking for food and water for our children. This is true for all Bushmen. . . . We do what we can and move forward. That is the Bushman's philosophy.

—Kaemme Teberi, female Bushmen healer and elder from Botswana, quoted in *Kalahari Bushmen Healers* by Bradford Keeney

I couldn't believe it—it actually worked. As I sat at the top of the hill at ALI near my classmates, suddenly we heard the forest come alive with bird calls and songs. Jonah had led us on a relatively long nature walk checking out animal tracks and looking and learning about trees. I think he was also trying to tire us out, so we might sit still. Once at the top of the hill, he prompted us to sit spread out from each other a little ways, stay still, and just listen. He promised if we waited long enough and were patient enough, then something special would happen. We sat fidgeting beneath the mixed hardwood forest, just far enough away from each other to not start whispering or causing trouble. After about 20 minutes we all heard it: a distinctive whistling sound with a slight trill.

We quietly huddled together with Jonah.

"That's a bobwhite. It's usually the first to begin calling again. But let's stay quiet and keep listening."

As we sat, more birds began to call, and there was even one I recognized.

"A cardinal!" I whispered in an excited voice.

Jonah nodded at me and put his finger to his lips as I continued to listen, chagrined.

Over the next 20 or so minutes, the simple calls of the bobwhite and the cardinal were joined by a complex chorus of many different birds and other animals. After we were able to sit still and be quiet in one place for some time, the forest simply came alive.

"It's like this everywhere in nature," Jonah explained, "but especially in a forest. People just don't sit still and quiet down for long enough to hear and even see the animals. The animals can hear us a mile away, and then they ditch and hide before we even get there. If you can quiet down and sit still, it will completely change your experience with animals. It's called quieting your concentric rings."

Jonah had learned this from reading Tom Brown's book, *The Tracker*, as a kid. Tom Brown's skills were something of a legend for the White family, similar to how Native scouts could hear and feel European colonizer armies coming from miles away by sensing the change in the birds in the forest. Little did I realize that, years after our hilltop bird adventure, I would dive deeply into these skills with a man who would share them with the world: Jon Young.

———

Understanding bird language and nature awareness stories is one of the best ways to understand the concept of *deep nature connection*, which is so very important as a survival skill. It is *the* foundational skill and forms the basis of many cultures' knowledge and connection to land and place. It's the primal precursor to other survival skills. Learning these bird language and deep nature connection skills under Jon shaped my awareness and understanding in huge and powerful ways that I am still unpacking and learning about. And they were a big part of my time as an Anake instructor at Wilderness Awareness School.

One morning, after a snowfall the previous night that left icy conditions at the school, Alexia and I were trying to determine how to proceed with class. Not all of our students had cellphones or access to e-mails, and they would often show up if they could (even if the roads were treacherous). Eventually, we decided to meet on Linne Doran at Malalo ya Chui, the fire pit and primary outdoor classroom on the land and assess the situation: How many students showed, how much snow and ice accumulated, and what could we do for the day? With a full third of the class missing and plenty of snow and ice on the land, we opted to throw out that day's planned curriculum.

It took a long time to get a friction fire that morning. The students were given the difficult challenge of having to start their fire on top of the snow, and then bring a coal into Malalo to start the central fire for the day. Several students were a little ticked at the scope and nature of the challenge, but after a blaze roared to life in the central fire pit everybody warmed up, both literally and emotionally.

We sent students out to do solo sits at their sit spots—the core areas where they spent the year deeply connecting to nature on an almost daily basis. We figured that sitting in the frozen winter wonderland would reveal a new understanding of the landscape to students, and it would also be a further survival challenge of how to stay comfortable under those circumstances. On top of that, we added in Jon's secret weapon to increase awareness, perception, and understanding: bird language.

As far as I know, Jon was the first to coin the term *bird language*, and he has been teaching about it for decades. Having written a book (*What the Robin Knows*), developed multiple study courses, and taught thousands of people over thousands of hours, Jon was still just scratching the surface of what birds can teach us about what's actually going on around us in nature.

The art of understanding bird language rose directly out of Jon's experience of doing many hours of sit spots under Tom Brown's mentoring, combined with an understanding of concentric rings, a concept passed on by Stalking Wolf. The concept of concentric rings in nature is quite simple but very profound. The basic version of it is that every disturbance and even movement in the woods puts off a ring of disturbance, much like when you drop a pebble in a pond. It starts with being quiet and still and extending your hearing. Next, you tune into all of your own senses and being to minimize your own concentric rings of movement and sound and read the rings of nature, figuring out not only where a disturbance was created, but also possibly what caused it.

Over time, Jon would synthesize bird language and the concept of concentric rings into a scientific and artistic approach. He developed a method to literally map over time what the birds were saying and doing, as witnessed by dozens of people. When putting together all the data and stories of a dozen or more people doing a bird language "sit" together, startling conclusions could be drawn about what was really going on in an area. This kind of deep understanding of the world around them was one of the key things that kept hunter-gatherer people alive. Paying attention to bird language can quickly turn our primal awareness and brains on.

So, the students went out with the dual challenge of keeping their asses from being frozen while also paying attention to what the birds were saying for an hour: the Anake program in a nutshell.

We called the students back in with a wolf howl, and they quickly returned to the relative warmth and comfort in Malalo. Huddled around the warm fire, we debriefed the students' bird "sit" as they wrote their observations, stories, maps, and pictures in their notebooks. Students described live sightings and audible sounds (both bird and otherwise) to people sitting near them during the "sit" to see where they overlapped, especially around significant events, including particularly loud noises or big disturbances. Once the small groups compared notes, we compiled the stories and data onto a master map in front of everybody. What ends up arising is a map full of twenty or more people's observations of a given area with key data points marked out. The data is keyed to represent the different time periods, and, thus, you have a map of time and space and everything that happened.

On that day, as Alexia and I put together the map and the stories, patterns began to emerge. It was very clear that there were two hotspots of activity that had occurred during the session. One was at a drainage on the northwest side of the pond, known as Death's Crossing (named by students from the WAS high school program: Community School). The spot was a known area for animal activity; the drainage created a landscape funnel where animals had to cross over from one part of the land to another. The other area was on the east side of the pond, in a more obscure and less traveled area. That spot was dense with brush, had a fair amount of slope, and was pretty hard to get to.

When we analyzed the information about the hotspots, we realized that there were significant sets of bird alarms and agitations in both spots during the middle portion of the bird sit. In the Death's Crossing area, the alarm sequence moved slowly across the area, with birds following whatever animal had moved through. The birds didn't seem extremely agitated but more annoyed, and this suggested a slow-moving animal. On the east side of the pond, however, it was a different story. The winter wrens had alarmed repeatedly in a small area with extreme agitation. They had formed a parabola shape around the animal causing the alarm, and they had alarmed for a significant chunk of time without moving.

After conferring with each other and asking the students some clarifying questions, Alexia and I were willing to put forth some guesses.

"Well . . . the alarms near Death's Crossing suggest a slower-moving animal, maybe a bear or a raccoon," Alexia began.

"And what about the east side of the pond? Anybody have thoughts on who was setting off the parabolic?" I asked the students.

A few hands went up, and then someone responded, "A weasel?"

"Yeah—that's a good guess. A weasel or someone in the weasel family." Alexia and I paused for dramatic effect. "Anybody up for a little snow tracking?"

The students hustled to gather their gear as we set out to go test out the morning's theories.

Not only had Jon developed the basic ideas of bird language and the method for mapping a group bird sit, he had, over time, seen and heard enough stories to be able to make highly accurate conjectures as to what caused the bird alarms. He could decode the patterns and stories and tell you if the jays were yelling about a bear or coyote, an owl or a hawk, or even a weasel. This kind of understanding and awareness is super practical. If the birds can alert you to dangerous animals, such as a large predator, or tell you where prey animals are (for potential food), then they can become allies in your primal journey. Alexia and I were putting into practice what we had learned from Jon, and now we were going to examine tracks in the snow to find out if we were right.

Alexia took the group to Death's Crossing, and I took the side of the pond with the way less sexy name: east side of the pond. My group consisted of a mixed bag of interest; some student were itching to get out to the eastern point and see what tracks were there, while others were content to explore mysteries in the snow along the way. There were even quite a few stragglers who simply wanted to throw snowballs at each other. I was leading my group from the front excited about what we might discover. Along the way, my group found amazing stories written in the snow: the tiny imprints of deer mouse feet, the minuscule tracks of juncos and winter wrens, and scattered Douglas fir cones that had been munched on by chipmunks trying to stay warm. Traveling along the side of the pond got rougher and rougher, and it soon became a combination of bushwhacking through snow-covered snowberry and salal bushes still covered with their large, leather-like green leaves and slipping and sliding at the awkward angle of the hillside. More and more students dropped off as the going got to be too tough, but a handful stayed with me, including Mink, a hardcore survival skills junkie who wanted to see if the tracks had been made by her namesake. After another 20 minutes, we found the general area where the parabolic alarms had come from. We split up and started searching as the sun began its rapid descent and it got significantly colder.

A few minutes after we split up, Mink and I spotted a collection of small tracks going into and out of a very narrow hole in the ground. We called the remainders of our group together and examined what we found. Soon it was clear that there were very small, very fresh tracks of a five-toed creature scurrying around the hole. The heel-pad and characteristic toe shape revealed to us that we had been right in our assessment: We had found weasel tracks right where we had heard the alarms!

While only a handful of students made it all the way out to that spot, the glee and excitement of our discovery was more than enough to carry us back to Malalo. There, we found that the other group had discovered raccoon tracks out at Death's Crossing that were also very, very fresh. By the time we wrapped up for the day, the students were lit up, excited by the discoveries, and expressing their wonder at the mysteries we had found and solved. Alexia and I enjoyed the warmth of the fire, the warmth of the students' excitement, and the joy of facilitating a fulfilling impromptu day. Maybe there really was something to this bird language stuff after all.

⌐ ⌐ ⌐

The world that Jon unlocked for me took all that I had learned at the Ancient Lifeways Institute, integrated it into an adult understanding, and propelled me on a continuous learning journey that would shape my life and others' lives to this very day. While it's safe to say that without my experience at ALI, this book would have never been written, I can also say that without Jon's influence and mentoring I wouldn't have been capable of writing this book.

These days, Jon Young has neck-length, salt-and-pepper hair, and his lean, Irish-Polish–American frame still bristles with energy, even though he is in his 50s. He travels around the world teaching, giving keynote speeches, writing, and running his organization, 8 Shields International, all while spearheading several other projects. I had the chance to sit down with him and get his insight into two of his favorite topics: deep nature connection and the primal wisdom and knowledge of the Kalahari Bushmen.

Perhaps it is Jon who can best describe what, exactly, deep nature connection truly is. *Deep nature connection* is a term Jon coined after an interaction with the editor of his book, *What the Robin Knows*, which combines storytelling, science, and Jon's insights to produce an introduction to bird language. His editor was skeptical about the message Jon was sharing. See, the editor had only known birders—who use a bird's sounds purely to identify the bird—and these birder contacts of his, who all had substantial influence in the conservation field, questioned the validity of what Jon was saying about the meaning of bird language. Birders are gifted naturalists and studiers of bird identification; they are also a powerful and significant part of conservation movements. However, not very many birders have really paid attention to *what birds are communicating to each other about their environment.* And, according to Jon, birds are actually continually communicating to each other about their environment, and are especially communicative about threats in their environment, such as predators.

One morning, Jon's book editor heard of a series of bird alarms followed by deep silence. Now, the editor was not a birder, but he knew based on what he had read and learned from Jon that this signaled the presence of a predator. In fact, it specifically signaled the appearance of an aerial predator—either a sharp-shinned hawk or a Cooper's hawk. He peeked his head outside and was stunned to see a Cooper's hawk sitting on a branch right outside his house. Immediately, the editor bought into Jon's theory of bird language and suggested to Jon he coin the term *deep bird language.*

Jon's research on the topic has been so compelling that there are now Bird Language Leader trainings being carried out across the country and the globe, including at several Audubon Centers (one of the largest birding organizations in the world) and his organization, 8 Shields.

While this experience while working on his book served to further validate Jon's work on bird language, it also gave him a term he had been searching for decades.

"Nate," Jon recalled with glee, "I walked right into a meeting with 8 Shields advisors and said to them, 'What we do is *deep nature connection!*'"

And so the term was born, and a movement was launched.

In 2005, Richard Louv published his book *Last Child in the Woods* in which he coined the term *Nature Deficit Disorder,* a phenomenon linked to ADD, ADHD, and other childhood sensory processing disorders. In his book, Richard put forth the very simple idea that children didn't need to be medicated for these conditions and simply needed to get outside and play in nature. I remember when this book came out, and how it became so much simpler to explain the work I was doing with children and adults. If Nature Deficit Disorder was the problem or illness, then nature connection was the solution.

But what about deep nature connection?

Over the years, many people have started to describe their work as a form of nature connection in relation to Louv's work, and while this is helpful, what Jon has been teaching and doing is a lot more in-depth, more long-term, and more sophisticated than what often happens during a 3-day overnight field trip in fifth grade to a local environmental education center for elementary school kids.

Jon also calls his work "strategic nature connection mentoring," likening deep nature connection work to what happens with a professional athlete. It's like a form of deeply structured and strategic primal awareness training.

"It's successive and progressive, Nate," he explained. "Deep nature connection work is work that takes our senses and sensory awareness to the next level. It creates a synergistic collaboration between our senses and the natural world. It's like training a pitcher in the major leagues and creating peak performance. You don't leave things to chance when training a professional athlete."

But why? Why do we need to do this? What is happening?

From what I've seen when using Jon's methods and system over the years, something deeply profound and astonishing happens when this strategic nature connection mentoring happens. Children and adults develop an entirely different relationship with the world around them. They end up having relationships with plants, birds, mammals, insects, trees, and other ecological species that most people aren't even aware of. As Jon puts it, in the ideal village of hunter-gatherers everyone is developing these kinds of relationships with everything in their environment. By the time they are 12 years old, they have a relationship with 400 different species. With some of these species they have a deeper relationship and with some, a lesser relationship, but they know and understand a huge amount about the natural world around them. These kinds of relationships are examples of the original primal relationships we humans have had with the natural world for most of our human existence.

For instance, it's important to know all of the poisonous plants, venomous animals, and other hazards in one's area. This isn't just to stay safe, but to actually be able to function in that environment without being paralyzed with fear and having one's nervous system shut down. I'm reminded of Nicole Apelian describing her ability to walk among black bears on Vancouver Island or change her tire out in the African bush with lions looking on. In both those situations, Nicole knew enough and had enough of a relationship with both bears and lions to assess the situation accurately and also to not have her nervous system freak out and create a truly dangerous situation through panicking.

Okay, but why would humans need to know over 400 different species in their bioregion?

Because that is what we have done for most of human history. Deep nature connection is actually the foundational and fundamental survival skill that forms the basis for all of the others. It's the original form of primal awareness and the core of the primal mind.

Or as Jon puts it, "Ya' know, the average reader or consumer of reality TV might think that survival training involves knowing how to use a few tools and being inventive. That's not what we are talking about. The San Bushmen of the Kalahari live in the most dangerous place on earth. Dehydration is a constant factor with temperatures of over 120 degrees Fahrenheit and no easy access to surface water. There are many different kinds of venomous snakes, lions, leopards, rogue male elephants, herds of cape buffalo sleeping nearby. There are so many ways to die. Machismo and super paranoia don't cut it out there."

For many in the survival skills world and the deep nature connection world, the Bushmen are the grandmasters. Jon, Nicole Apelian, and Stone Age expert Lynx Vilden have all spent time learning and studying with these modern-day Stone Age hunter-gatherer nomad experts.

If you want to understand what *primal* really means or what is happening underneath our veneer of civilization, then you should know who the Bushmen are. In many undergraduate anthropology classes across the world, the Bushmen are looked at as living, surviving examples of who we were as our most ancient selves. Known sometimes as the San, Basarwa, or Khwe, the Bushmen are indigenous hunter-gatherers who live in the very harsh realm of the Kalahari Desert. The Bushmen live in countries such as Botswana, Namibia, South Africa, Zambia, Zimbabwe, and Angola. While there are very few who live fully hunter-gatherer lives in the face of severe pressure from modernity in Africa, there are bands of Bushmen who live similarly to how their ancestors did 60,000 years ago. Rock art in parts of South Africa that has been dated back to that time depicts what looks like Bushmen engaging in ceremonies, dancing, and other practices still present today. They truly are the grandmasters of survival and deep nature connection.

As Jon puts it, to simply survive in the Kalahari as a teenager you have to have a PhD in deep nature connection. Here's an example: In some popular film footage, a Bushman hunter-tracker wanders out away from his village. Suddenly, there is a cobra nearby. Without hesitation or nervousness, the Bushman hunter grabs the snake by the tail, whips it super hard, and simply cracks it neck. The threat is neutralized and turned into a meal, with no change in demeanor or stress level.

"It's like they're master musicians or sports stars," Jon mused. "If I wanted to learn to play the fiddle better like I wanted to in my late teens, I would hang around a masterful fiddle player. For a short while, I would play significantly better," Jon shared.

"The Bushmen are totally at ease in what we would consider a hostile environment. They make it look easy. They have a deep relationship with the world around them. It reminds me of spending time with Victor Wooten [a world-class bass player]. He's on his game, he doesn't have to think about. He just relies on his neuromuscular patterning, like an amazing sports performer."

Jon spends time with the Bushmen every year. For Bushmen, it's not survival—it's simply living. If the Bushmen weren't masters of deep nature connection and bird language, they couldn't live where and how they live. Bird language provides continuous feedback about dangers and potential food sources, while tracking does the same thing on the ground. In fact, Jon feels that tracking and bird language are the two skills that most quickly develop deep nature connection and form the foundation for what we call survival skills.

Going Deeper

Jon Young was the founder of Wilderness Awareness School, which he started in New Jersey in 1983. The school moved to Washington State, and I became one of the junior instructors there when Jon was still very involved. Later, Jon departed to share his teachings to an even bigger audience both nationally and worldwide. His legacy lives on in programs like Anake, and the power of his methods, approaches, and understanding allows people like me and my fellow instructors to blossom and grow a robust, vibrant transformational program and school.

Jon grew up under the wing of Tom Brown Jr. (see page 10). The two of them met when Tom was 21 and Jon was 10. Their adventures and journeys together paralleled Tom's own upbringing under an Apache elder named Stalking Wolf, and whom Tom called Grandfather. The stories of these adventures served as the blueprint for the epic nature programs that Wilderness Awareness School ran for decades for both youth and adults from all walks of life. Bird language was just one of many core areas of study as WAS became the center of deep nature connection education for adults and children.

If you want to know about bird language, one of the best places to start is Jon's book *What the Robin Knows*. One of his other books *Coyote's Guide to Connecting with Nature* is basically an instructional manual on deep nature connection that's especially useful for mentors, educators, and parents. He's also created several audio and online resources through his organization 8 Shields. 8 Shields media and 8Shields.org have lots of resources available for training deep nature connection and bird language, and it is here where you can learn more about Jon's latest work. Dan Gardoqui, one of Jon's first students and the founder of White Pine Programs in Maine, is another highly trained expert and teacher in bird language. He teaches classes there and across the country. Kristi Dranginis, a WAS alumna, has also created a distance learning program for learning the birds in your area called Bird Mentor, available at birdmentor.com. If you want to learn more about the Bushmen, there are lots of good resources out there, but I highly recommend the work of Bradford Keeney, including the book *Ropes to God*. Rupert Isaacson, the author of *Horse Boy* and the creator of the film by the same name, has also spent a lot of time with the Bushmen and has written of his adventures. Finally, the film *The Great Dance* gives a deep look at Bushmen lives as they try to hold onto their traditional culture in the face of cultural change.

And, unlike so many of the shows we see on television, this is not a solo endeavor. Deep nature connection works much better and happens much better with a group undergoing the same process, like in the previously mentioned Bird Language Leaders programs or the Anake program or a Bushmen Village.

What are the benefits of immersing oneself in these deep nature connection practices? What happens to our brain if we spend unstructured time in nature with intact healthy ecosystems around us? What happens if we develop that relationship with up to 400 species in our local environment?

According to Richard Louv, it's pretty simple: We become happier, healthier, and smarter. In his follow-up works to *Last Child in the Woods*, Louv shows that adults, children, seniors— really, all of us—need lots of time in nature to be happy, healthy functioning humans. He even coined a term for this: *Vitamin N*, the title of one of his books and his way of describing how important nature is. And, while not everyone has the desire or ability to immediately start practicing survival skills, such as fire-making or shelter-building, bird language and other forms of deep nature connection are available to all of us all the time in our own bioregion. This makes unlocking our primal nature and remembering our hunter-gatherer roots a practice we can all access almost anywhere. Spending time in nature is something we can all do, at least a little bit, every day.

Louv is not alone. Author Florence Williams has looked deeply into this topic with her book, *The Nature Fix*. In her work, Williams explores why and how so many of our greatest inventors and most creative people drew their inspiration from nature. She looks at Beethoven, Wordsworth, Tesla, and others, while also traveling around the world to look at nature connection in different settings. Her conclusions are similar to Louv's: time in nature promotes a better mood, better health, and better creativity. And there is plenty of science to back all of this up.

About a decade ago I was supervising instructors running a summer camp for kids on Cougar Mountain in Issaquah, Washington. The program was pretty basic but super enjoyable: have the kids participate in deep nature connection games, wanders, and nature activities, and learn the basics of survival. They did this all day, every day, under the guidance of experienced mentors. Many parents described it as one of the best summer camps ever. After a morning of sign-in and storytelling, the groups dispersed to the woods on adventures. But one mother approached me to chat.

She relayed to me how excited she was about what we were doing, but she was also excited to share about her work as a graduate student working on her PhD in neurobiology. One of the reasons she was so excited was because of the changes in her field.

"Nate, not that long ago at a neurobiology conference there might be one paper out of a hundred about nature and the human brain. Now, at the last conference I went to, there were over fifty papers about nature and the brain—and the numbers are growing!"

I didn't realize it at the time, but that parent was sharing information that would make my job easier in many ways over the next 10 years. Simply put, more science backed up this simple premise: Our brains thrive when in nature.

This might seem like a rhetorical question, but why?

The answer is stunning in its simplicity and its implications:

Our brain is designed to function best in the multifaceted, multisensory stimulating world of nature filled with plants, birds, trees, mammals, insects, fungi, and so on. We spent almost all of human history spending vast amounts of time in nature every day. Our brains have not evolutionarily caught up with the changes we've created in our human environment.

Well, what happens when we don't get enough time in nature?

The opposite of what happens when we get enough of our vitamin N: depression, anxiety, stress, angst, feelings of being overwhelmed, issues with obesity, problems with our biorhythms, and potentially something that is appearing more than ever: sensory processing disorders such as ADHD/ADD, and others. We and our kids may not need more medication, we may just need time outside. (This is something we will look at more in depth in Chapter 8.)

For instance, Kathleen Lockyear is an occupational therapist and mom who uses this approach as her *primary* way to help kids and their families as they struggle with autism, ADHD, ADD, and other related challenges. Her work is called Rx Outside or "prescription outside," with the notion that just being outside can make a huge difference in what we are now perceiving as disorders. Kathleen points out staggering numbers like the fact that 23.5 percent of children are now on at least one prescription drug daily, or that the average child spends only 7 percent of their time outside daily.

We will continue to come back to this theme over the next few chapters. For now, I can say that there is a growing field of specialists who are using deep nature connection to treat a whole array of disorders.

There are also highly trained experts and academics now looking at the impact of time in nature in human development and how it influences who we are for our whole life. Dr. Darcia Narvaez, a psychology professor at the University of Notre Dame, has researched for decades the relationship between human morality, human development, parenting, and healthy child-rearing. Her recent research has focused on small bands of hunter-gatherers and the kinds of human development that happens in these kinds of groups that mimic the earliest social groupings of humanity.

Her results and conclusions are quite powerful. One of her basic ideas is that our morality is actually heavily based on our neurobiology, not on ideas that we encounter throughout life. And our neurobiology is heavily based on how we were raised as children and what environment we interacted with from the earliest age. She points out that, for 99 percent of human existence, we were in small hunter-gatherer groups in a natural setting and that the neurobiology of our brain is expecting that. It might even be critical to developing a normal, morally functioning human being.

I'm going to restate that and repeat it just so we're clear: *Dr. Narvaez has basically shown that our brains are expecting to be raised as hunter-gatherer nomads and that, if we aren't, it can have serious impacts on our social and psychological development as humans.*

This is another reason why Jon spends so much time visiting with, developing relationships with, and studying with the Bushmen; it's not just that they are grandmasters of deep nature connection, but that they are grandmasters of natural human development, morality, and wisdom.

In the village in which Jon works, there are sixty to seventy people of all ages with a deep level of connection with and awareness of each other and their local environment. Jon quickly noticed that his "strategic nature connecting mentoring" was happening all the time throughout the village in a multigenerational fluid, effortless way. Aunts, uncles, grandparents, and even older kids worked together seamlessly to help facilitate the next generation of PhDs in deep nature connection—and they didn't even realize they were doing it.

Our own culture is often invisible to us as it is the context in which we operate. From Jon's observations, it appeared to be the same with the San Bushmen—they were unconsciously competent at passing on and developing immense knowledge, wisdom, and relationship to place. This permitted their children to grow into healthy functioning young adults who could easily survive in one of the most hostile environments on the planet. Original primal hunter-gatherer training and awareness happened all the time for everyone.

Jon has now spent years going back to the same village working with the same people learning how and why they do what they do, all so he can improve the work of deep nature connection that is happening all over the globe at schools like Wilderness Awareness School and through his organization, 8 Shields. One of the surprising things Jon found is that at first the Bushmen were incredulous that this wasn't already happening everywhere. In fact, they had trouble believing people could actually survive without deep nature connection or *if they could even be people.*

I wanted to know more about what the Bushmen think of the fact that deep nature connection or rather deep nature *reconnection* is happening all over the world. Jon shared a story about this from one of his recent trips.

"I asked them about this, and they got really, really reflective. There was a lot of talk back and forth, and the translator told me that I had really stirred the pot by telling them about this work going around the world. Finally, one old grandmother summed it up by saying, 'Do you mean that by simply being ourselves, we are helping the world?'"

Jon applied in the affirmative, and members of the Bushmen village got really excited. They suddenly wanted Jon and his crew to bring their video cameras and microphones with them to follow the Bushmen around and to ask questions about what they were doing.

"If doing that helps other parents and children and kids, we really want to help," shared another Bushmen tribal member.

Jon has taken this invitation and run with it. In 2018, he and Nicole Apelian launched the 8 Shields Origins Project, which seeks to bring Bushmen mentoring, deep nature connection practices, child-rearing skills, and culture to the rest of the world as a potential antidote to many of the challenges we face.

For the Bushmen to be encouraged and actively supported in living their traditional lifestyle, with their wisdom and teaching going out to create positive change in the world, is a huge change for them. Often, they faced immense pressure, sometimes backed by government-sponsored violence, to give up their way of life and conform and live in cramped shanty villages afflicted with poverty, violence, and exploitation.

Realizing that there is something that they have to offer to the rest of the world by simply being who they are and keeping alive our original human model gives great hope to the Bushmen, and possibly to the rest of us, as well. While we might not all want to live the traditional Bushmen lifestyle, it is possible that these forms of deep nature connection can help all of us in deepening our own primal awareness and increase our quality of life.

During my time as the program director of WAS, I was able to bring Jon up for different inspiring workshops: The Sacred Hunt, Intuitive Animal Tracking, Bird Language, and more. For a recent workshop, I urged Jon to share what he had learned and gathered from his trips and time with the Bushmen. We talked about deep nature connection, cords or ropes of connection, trance-dance healing, and what the Bushmen wanted to share with an American audience.

During the Bushman workshop, Jon shared the story about one of his most patient and diligent students who over the years had spent countless hours practicing the bird language routines and teachings Jon had given. This student described experiencing the landscape as a honeycomb with pockets of normal activity punctuated with "holes" in the honeycomb of disturbance that he could read. This student even used this understanding to help a family find a lost dog in the area where he regularly did his sit spot activity. He was able to pinpoint where the dog was from almost a mile away, just from reading what the birds were doing. This was a clear example of bringing ancient practices into a modern context to help people alleviate a stressful situation.

After the Bushman workshop, Jon and I remarked that it was a remarkable story that his student had shared. It was impressive to know one's sit spot area to such a deep degree that you could tell exactly where an animal was—and from so far away.

I dropped Jon off at the airport on that Sunday afternoon after the workshop. The next morning, I headed down to my own sit spot to enjoy some relaxing deep nature connection. Only, everything was completely different. Suddenly, only about 10 yards from my front door, I could hear and pay attention to areas of bird language and animal behavior way beyond the scope of what I normally was able to do. I found myself unconsciously scanning the honeycomb landscape in a deeper and more intricate way than I had ever before. I'd been practicing bird language for years—decades, even—at this point, and, yet, one weekend with Jon, and he'd opened my mind and awareness to a whole new level. Seeing and hearing the landscape through this primal lens gave me a hint of what it must be like to have the hunter-gatherer level of awareness of the Bushmen people.

The impact that Jon Young and Tom Brown Jr. have had on me, Wilderness Awareness School, outdoor education, and the survival skills movement cannot be overstated, and I think it is vastly underestimated. Between the two of them, they have fundamentally changed the face of environmental education in many parts of the world, helped spread survival skills all over the world, and, specifically, have had a huge impact on bringing to the forefront the deeper aspects of some of the "soft" survival skills, such as awareness training, tracking, bird language, and developing intuition. These kinds of primal awareness skills are often forgotten and not considered to be as important as other hands-on survival skills.

In his book, *The Raven's Gift*, Jon Turk shares his idea that most hunter-gatherer and nomadic peoples that are deeply nature connected are primarily right-brain focused. He shares how our modern education, economic, and living system constantly engages our left-brained thinking, analyzing, and abstracting aspects of being, and how being in a wilderness setting under dangerous conditions you automatically drop into the awareness-oriented, right-brained aspect of yourself. He saw this quite prominently among the Koryak people, whom he spent time with in the Kamchatka peninsula, and especially among those who still actively herded reindeer as part of their existence.

We often forget how important deep nature connection is as a survival skill. It is *the* foundational skill and formed the basis of many cultures' knowledge and connection to land and place. It is one of many primal skills that allowed our ancestors to survive, one of many that still linger latently in our brain and awareness. And, as Nicole Apelian shared earlier with her stories of lions, wolves, cougars, and bears (oh my), *if we aren't paying attention with a lot of awareness, then we could get eaten.* It doesn't really matter at that point how good your fire-making skills are or how good you are at building a shelter.

CHAPTER 6

The Reindigenization of the Soul: Native Perspectives on the Survival Skills Movement

In the settler mind, land was property, real estate, capital, or natural resources. But to our people, it was everything: identity, the connection to our ancestors, the home of our nonhuman kinfolk, our pharmacy, our library, the source of all that sustained us.

—FROM *BRAIDING SWEETGRASS*,
BY ROBIN WALL KIMMERER, POTAWATOMI TRIBAL
MEMBER, SCIENTIST, PROFESSOR, AND MOTHER

IN THE GREATER CONTEXT OF RETURNING TO OUR PRIMAL ROOTS, we must explore the idea of what our roots truly are. Where do we come from? Who are we really? Who were our primal ancestors? How did they live and what did they do? Exploring these questions and finding answers sometimes means taking a hard look at culture, tradition, and especially the history and condition of the Native people on the land we now live on. At one time, we were all indigenous to somewhere, but time and history have moved people all around the globe. As we discover our primal ancestry, we may naturally become curious about contemporary hunter-gatherer people or indigenous people and how they live.

Asking, exploring, and discovering their stories of who they are and what deep nature connection is might shed some light for all of us. Their answers may surprise, and we may find ourselves bumping up against uncomfortable and complicated truths about history and the places we now call home. In my experience, indigenous teachers have a lot to offer the survival skills movement and those exploring their primal nature, and one of the things they most commonly share is that our original human nature is more than just skills and nature connection. Culture is a vital part of the wild human experience and storytelling, song, ceremony, and dance may be just as important as knowing how to make a fire.

When I was at ALI, while I learned all sorts of physical skills, another key teaching was what John called "oral tradition." It would be easy to simplify this aspect of what was shared there and simply call it "storytelling around the fire" each night. But John was very deliberate in calling our evening time something other than just storytelling. Oral tradition implies something going back, way back, and it also implies continuity, connection, and lineage.

Each night, after the sun had gone down, we gathered around a fire in Kaskaskia Lodge, and John shared stories that he had heard from Native American elders, some of which were part of his own family and lineage and some of which had been shared and collected from elsewhere. The stories were phenomenal, and John was an incredible storyteller. Later, as a teacher and mentor of others, I would share stories, and any talent or skill I displayed in doing this I attribute to being exposed to the deep rhythm, cadence, and connection that John had in his oral tradition sharing.

John's stories were truly epic, and they often contained potent teachings, wisdom, and information that related to what we were doing, or had been learning, in the last few days. Some of the stories were quite old; one of the stories I remember most clearly was about hunters' breaking a sacred rule by refusing to offer thanks to the animal they hunted. In the story, the animals pray to the Creator for help, and the Creator sends a mammoth to defend the animals' honor and to teach the human village a lesson. It's estimated that mammoths went extinct approximately 10,000 years ago, and there is every possibility that the story was at least that old.

Other stories John shared connected to the themes we've looked at so far in this book, including a beautiful story about the origin of fire and a spider teaching people to breathe a coal into life, stories of an old woman standing up to a band of armed warriors threatening her village, and the story of a warrior named Blue Jay who had lost his sight but could still use his hearing to navigate as a hunter and protector for his village.

It took me a long time to realize how lucky I was to be exposed to John, his teachings, and especially his stories. When you are a teenager, it's pretty easy to assume that everybody else in the world is having an experience similar to what you are having. I started to get hints that what we were experiencing at ALI was something special when John shared a story of his own life regarding the oral traditions he carried. While I cherish the time I had at ALI making fire, creating stone tools, making pottery out of clay dug from the earth, and running through the forest wild and free, John's stories and our oral tradition time were just as potent and important.

As a graduate student, John spent part of his time doing fieldwork collecting stories from Native elders in his network. During this time, John hand-wrote most of these stories and created a huge paper archive of what had previously been a completely oral system of storytelling and native wisdom. Unfortunately, all of the paper files John had collected were completely lost and destroyed in a fire.

I know I still wonder at what was lost in that fire, but I really listened when John told us that he took this as a sign. For him, this was a clear message that those stories, that wisdom, that lore was not meant to be written down. What had been an oral tradition should remain an oral tradition, and from that time on John did not write down the stories he learned. He simply passed them on through word-of-mouth around a fire, as they had been passed for thousands of years.

The skills we learned at ALI were ancestral human skills. Fire-making, hide-working, flintknapping, making pottery, and even storytelling were skills that everyone's ancestors needed to survive. We were not "playing Indian" or even learning a specific Cherokee or other Native American way of doing things. In fact, the skills we were learning and doing pointed at a core human way of life that emphasized *our common humanity*. Teachings and wisdom from other cultures were mixed in, from Greek to Mesopotamian to Celtic.

But, while most of the people in the field of survival skills, deep nature connection, and related arts have a similar mindset about the skills they're learning, some people want to explore their fantasies about living like a Native American or becoming indigenous. Often, these people are white, from a pretty privileged background, and with very little awareness or understanding of the historical complexity of the United States. There is a huge cultural void in America regarding the darkness that played out when European settlers and colonizers arrived here and perpetuated deliberate genocide and mass deception to take this land from the Native indigenous inhabitants who had been here for thousands and perhaps tens of thousands of years.

To add further layers to the complexity of the teachings, many of the people who teach these skills and arts are white European Americans who often have a teaching connection or lineage related to specific Native North American teachers. This can easily create an aura of cultural appropriation, or of white people continuing to perpetuate colonialism by benefiting from the indigenous arts and teachings of this continent. Over the last

5 to 10 years, a conversation around this conundrum has begun to arise and flourish in the survival skills and deep nature connection world. As this primal movement has grown exponentially, rich dialogue, difficult questions, and new ways of presenting and sharing that don't shy away from these complex issues are emerging. At the same time, more people of color, people of indigenous ancestry, and other diverse populations are finding their way into the survival skills movement and going on their own primal journeys, adding their voices, questions, and ideas to produce a rich dialogue and interaction.

The arising diversity and critical questions within this movement parallels bigger questions facing our nation and the world. At this moment, there is tremendous tension, challenge, and conflict around indigenous representation, voice, and perspective. The protest and standoff at Standing Rock over water rights, for example, is just one of many contemporary hotspots where these unresolved issues are coming out. These are not easy issues to tackle, and there are no easy direct answers. Being a core teacher of primal human skills and ways of life, I don't have the luxury of shying away from these difficult questions and issues.

Indigenous teachers and Native North American elders have directly played a role in my growth as a mature adult and have had a huge impact on my development as an instructor of deep nature connection, survival skills, natural movement, herbal medicine, and related arts. For the most part, these elders, teachers, storytellers, and cultural bearers came into my life at WAS after learning more about the school's teachings and program. Some of these elders even took classes and began taking teachings back from WAS to their own communities, starting tracking clubs or sharing survival skills with their own people.

Many Native teachers have a sustained curiosity about and desire to contribute to organizations like WAS because they saw firsthand the power of people deeply connecting to nature and unlocking their primal nature. But they also saw it as their responsibility to ensure that the more subtle and equally important primal skills of storytelling, ceremony, dance, conflict resolution, and culture were not neglected. In many ways, Native teachers and leaders became a core part of this growing exploration of our primal human nature. Heck, John White, the founder of ALI, was one of the pioneers of the movement. Why were these teachers drawn to join this growing primal roots movement in their own unique way? And, how can we all reconcile issues such as cultural appropriation, decolonization, and the history that so many are reluctant to face? What are Native perspectives on deep nature connection, our primal journey, and survival skills, both in the past and currently?

There are many different answers. Some saw something special happening with the students at WAS when they got deeply connected to nature and immersed themselves in ancestral skills. Their hope was to bring these kinds of learning moments back to their own communities and people. Others see what's happening with the survival skills and deep nature connection movement as a fulfillment of prophecies within their own culture. These prophecies describe "earth changes" that we are on the verge of and emphasize the importance of relearning ancestral skills. These "earth change" prophecies forecast imminent environmental disaster or collapse if modern humans don't learn to change their conduct and relationship to the natural world. Some of these prophecies speak specifically of people needing to relearn ancient survival skills, as our modern infrastructure is likely to dissolve and go away if we don't change how we are living.

Indigenous teachers are now sharing, learning, and taking things back to their own people, even in the face of big challenges in their own communities, such as a high rates of suicide and fetal alcohol syndrome, and a growing number of missing Native women. And they are not hesitant to directly address the big issues and ideas of cultural appropriation, decolonization, and even the idea of reindigenization.

Tony Ten Fingers is one such teacher and leader. Tony was born and raised in Oglala, South Dakota, and was a significant contributor to the early days of the primal movement, especially on the East Coast. He has worked across the country helping people heal from trauma by connecting deeply to nature. He has served as a mentor to these people and has done ground-breaking work on suicide prevention in Native communities. He has also personally experienced the impact of youth suicide on reservations, having lost family members to the epidemic. I know Tony from my early days at WAS, and he is always a solid presence of warmth, kindness, insight, and deep heartfelt sharing. When I first met Tony, he had the appearance of many archetypal images of Lakota people: strong, long vibrant black hair, and a prominent hawk-like nose. Tony's Lakota name is *Wanbli Nata'u*, which means Raging Eagle. The irony is that Tony never rages at anybody; he maintains a peaceful, ironic, and quite funny demeanor.

Much of Tony's work and the work that he sees happening through survival skills, the primal journey, and deep nature connection is about establishing Identity, especially for Native people. Whether it's working with troubled teen youth in a wilderness setting, playing with elementary school kids on the reservation, or doing suicide prevention, a lot comes back to knowing who we are. We need to learn to know who we really are and to identify or even re-identify who we are. Tony sees survival skills as one valid path for this quest, and it's important to realize that all people long to be connected to their deep primal nature.

So what, exactly, is the connection between survival skills and finding one's identity?

"When we're in nature practicing survival skills, that's when things make sense in the world," said Tony. "It's not because we sit at a computer or use Google to identify what we need. We go into nature, and we bow-drill a fire because we need to stay warm or cook our food."

Spending a day outside is when we strip everything down to the bare essentials, and the hyperactive nature of our minds and egos start to melt away.

"In the bigger picture, [when practicing survival skills] at the end of the day you realize what a beautiful day it's been. There's a much bigger picture at play. That's the spiritual nourishment we need that's lacking in the world," Tony summarized.

Tony's view of the interconnectedness between nature and spirituality is a theme often endorsed by indigenous teachers. While it may fall into some people's stereotypical notions of Native Americans, many of the Native people I've encountered have emphasized the importance of the spiritual aspect of what happens when people spend time in nature or practice survival skills. It's almost like there's an inherent primal spiritual way of seeing the world that emerges from doing these skills. I've experienced this directly, as have my friends and family, and a natural, elegant spiritual fulfillment often comes from exploring primal nature and a deep connection to the natural world.

Science also shows that a lack of nature (or nature deficit) leads to a greater sense of disharmony in our lives and on our planet. As mentioned before, Richard Louv has documented this extensively in his work, including in his book *Vitamin N*. Louv equates nature with an essential nutrient that we need to thrive, be happy, and healthy for both children and adults. Tony agrees and sees a direct relationship to all the turmoil in our society with our disconnection from nature—everything from mass shootings to extreme weather to the anxiety and depression troubling our youth.

"If everyone practiced going out in nature 2 to 3 days a week or even just every weekend, then those disruptions would not happen. Our lack of spiritual nourishment [from nature] is the seed for the disruptions of hate, injustice . . . we have problems with these things because our spirit isn't fed," Tony said.

Tony knew me when I was in my early 20s and just starting to be a part of this primal movement. He doesn't hesitate to remind me of the impacts that this work immersion have had on my life.

"When I started doing this work years ago back in New Jersey, I started to see the bigger picture about the impacts on our lives. You are a product of this kind of work, Nate. You are a result of learning all these things . . . it's shaped what kind of man you are, what kind of family man you are, what kind of man you are in the community. Just like it's shaped me."

This was in a lot of ways a pointed reminder to me of my own privilege around these experiences and helped me remember how lucky I had been to have these experiences a part of my life for some time.

But what about Native communities? What about the children and adults on the reservation? What kind of opportunities for nature connection are there?

Many of the traditional spiritual practices of Lakota culture are intimately tied to nature and connection and are intended to connect them to their primal roots and ancestors. For instance, the *Innipi*, or sweat lodge, is a purification ceremony that incorporates many different elements from nature, including stones harvested from riverbanks, plants (such as sage and sweetgrass), water held in traditional gourd dippers, and the lodge itself, which is built from sixteen different willow poles. Every *Innipi* ceremony is an example of people practicing survival skills by harvesting plants, rocks, and other elements from their own land. Through the ceremony, they develop relationships with those natural elements, and it's a form of deep primal remembrance stretching back to ancestral hunter-gatherer days before the era of colonization.

Similar things hold true for the Sun Dance, a once-a-year major religious and spiritual ceremony at the center of Lakota spiritual tradition. The Sun Dance is a multiday event. The dance, which takes place on a flat, wide-open plain, requires enormous understanding of local ecology, plants, wood, wind, weather, and materials to be successfully pulled off. Everything must be harvested and prepared in a specific way that goes back to ancestral, primal times. Even the *Hanbleychya*, or what many people know as a vision quest (or vision fast), is a nature-based practice of spending 4 days and nights in isolation in nature to focus on praying for all the elements of the natural world around you—a deep nature connection practice for sure. For modern people rediscovering their own ancestral roots and primal nature, the intact cultural and environmental relationships present in the Sun Dance or vision fast can demonstrate what happens when a people hold true to their own primal journey.

I wanted to get Tony's specific thoughts and insights on colonization and decolonization—a conversation at the heart of many Native communities and their allies right now, and important for anyone starting to rediscover their own primal longings and nature.

Tony brought up the simple act of putting your feet in wild water. This is a tactic he frequently used as a way to work with teens in wilderness therapy. Often, teens in these programs have become numbed out emotionally due to trauma or abuse or addiction. In this exercise, the water helps them feel again and become reacquainted with the wonder of natural sensation.

"With young people, we take them to a stream and have them experience it and feel it. [Have them] touch the water and wade in it [and] start identifying with that feeling, it doesn't matter if it's an ice-cold brook or warm springs. The feelings are what matters . . . that's what matters in the world."

"If a person feels that doing [this exercise] is nonsense, then they've been colonized. You have to decolonize them, and you have to learn to communicate with them about this. Where does something like that come from? Maybe from their parents and upbringing. Maybe they learned it is nonsense to stay in the stream, and maybe they've been working from 8 to 5 for too long. To decolonize, you must help people feel good in their heart."

I've seen this numbness time and time again. Sometimes, it's fear or the shame of getting dirty. It might even be shame at wanting to play or even being outside. But when people spend time really feeling and being, that numbness starts to melt away.

"Colonization and decolonization are both a process. In Lakota, we talk about *Dankuskanskan*—a natural process. The river is a natural process, it goes where there's the least resistance. Rain from the clouds falls to the earth and runs into the river and then flows into the ocean. This cycle is *Dankuskanskan*, and decolonization is a process that we need to learn. How does it work for the people in power, and how does it work for those that are oppressed?" Tony said.

Tony emphasized how important it is to do this kind of work and how people who are colonized become so wrapped up in the material world, the work world, and media that their lives revolve around traffic jams, money-making opportunities, and the negative stories on the news. He really believes that there are answers to these problems through these natural practices.

"When someone does *Hanbleychya*, a vision quest, you go out there for 4 days and nights, below the stars at night. You see a bigger picture, and are not so colonized. The end result is that [the person] usually sheds tears. It doesn't matter who they are or where they're from, they shed tears—not tears of sadness, but tears of beauty . . . of the beauty of life."

This was what Tony saw as decolonization: melting our hearts so that we can feel again and unplugging ourselves from the continual high-stimulation of the modern material world.

When I asked Tony about what is needed on the reservation, he didn't hesitate: "Mentoring, more mentoring. We have the ceremonies and a lot of language and culture. But we could use more mentoring."

Tony grew up being mentored by his grandmother. While his older siblings faced the realities of boarding school on the reservation (where their language and culture was systematically oppressed), Tony was dropped off by his dad to spend time with his grandmother. A traditional woman who spoke fluent Lakota,

English, and Cheyenne and did things the old way, she would sit under a tree with Tony and make moccasins without needle and thread. The two of them would gather and dry plums, chokecherries, and wild turnips. And at night, when Tony stayed over, she shared stories of the buffalo nation, the deer nation, and the eagle nation. These stories stayed with him and informed his work to this day. Their bond was so strong that when the two of them were apart, if Tony willed it, she would show up in his dreams. This is an example of primal culture, skills, and knowledge being transferred from generation to generation, and what Tony describes in his relationship with his grandmother is what many people long for. Tony's primal awakening and connection to his own people's roots wasn't just about gathering wild foods and making moccasins; it also included sharing stories and establishing deep relationships. It's also very similar to what Tamarack Song and Tom Elpel share of their own awakening to a primal world through time spent with their own savvy, nature-connected grandmothers.

Tony carries on this tradition of passing down the old ways today by sharing it with others. He told me of how, when he returned to the reservation, he was asked by a family to participate in a special ceremony with their soon-to-be-born child. Tony was asked to be present at the birth and to share his breath, or *Ni*, with the child to form a bond and to pass on some of his strength and attributes. Tony accepted, and was quite surprised when, while he was at a conference over 100 miles away, the call came to announce that labor had started. Tony drove the 100-plus miles to the reservation in the middle of a snowstorm to be present at the birth of his new "nephew," Jesse James. The ceremony was performed on time, and Tony and Jesse James have been close ever since.

Even when Jesse James was little, he crawled after Tony, following his every footstep. Jesse is in sixth grade now; for Tony, it's critical for him to be a mentor and role model for Jesse James and to be in his life. And now Jada, Jesse James's little sister, is getting in on the action, as well. When they all get together, they tell stories and ask questions and play. Jada likes to wear Tony's hat while she's with him and will only give it away when it's time for Tony to leave. Tony is carrying on his people's primal traditions by honoring the ceremony he was asked to participate in and taking on a cultural leadership role with Jesse and Jada.

Tony's stories give me hope. They remind me of the importance of human relationships and the importance of culture for people. They give insight into the wisdom and mentoring that Tony's grandmother passed on to him and which he subsequently passed on to young people in his community. Far too often, people think that survival skills, like making fire or setting traps or learning to skin animals, is what our primal selves long for. This may be the case. But, telling stories, playing, mentoring, and connecting are all ancient primal parts of being human. These are just as important for survival and serve to nourish our primal nature just as much as making fire. They may also be one of the most powerful forms of decolonization any of us can undertake.

Native Teachers and Indigenous Revival in the Primal Movement

Over the years, a number of teachers have openly taught, shared, and learned with people practicing survival skills and deep nature connection. Gilbert Walking Bull, a Lakota elder, lived on the WAS home base property and openly taught and shared with both students and staff. Jake Swamp, who was a sub-chief of the Wolf Clan of the Mohawk people, regularly visited WAS and other deep nature connection organizations and taught his people's tradition of peacemaking and conflict resolution. Odawa teacher Paul Raphael shared the importance of elders in a cohesive, healthy culture, and actively pushed WAS and other groups to find a role for elders within the school and programs. Ralph Bennett, a Haida carver and storyteller, taught some of the first generation of high school–age students at WAS. Other significant teachers include Barry Moses, who spent time at Twin Eagles Wilderness School, and Juan Villuero, who joined the Children of the Earth Foundation. Local Lummi storyteller Swil Kanim became a regular contributor to the Anake program.

Native communities across the globe see a growing interest in, rediscovery of, and collaboration around their own traditional survival skills and primal connection. One program, named Rediscovery, has camps all across North America where Native youth can come and learn traditional skills from Native elders and teachers in traditional settings. Gene Tagaban has run a similar program in the summer time for the Nisqually people, bringing in teachers and experts from survival immersion programs. In other places, non-Native teachers have developed connections and relationships with Native communities over time and slowly built relationships that have allowed survival skills to be shared. Programs like Matt Kirk's Kauai Nature School on the island of Kauai and Steve Leckman's Coyote Programmes in Montreal serve both Native and non-Native groups, and Steve has an ongoing collaboration with the Mohawk people. Sal Gencarelle worked with WAS grad Matt McKinney to run Language of the Land, a traditional skills program for Lakota youth on the Pine Ridge reservation. Bill McConnell, a former instructor at Tom Brown's Tracker School who has been on the show *Dual Survival*, has been teaching traditional survival skills to the Apache people since 2005.

Gene Tagaban is a traditional Raven-dancer (someone who dresses, dances, and embodies the character of Raven during storytelling and dance performances), and he looks the part. With his striking long hair, prominent nose, and sharp features, Gene looks a lot like Raven. Not raven, the bird, but archetypal, mythological Raven. He's a very gifted storyteller, mentor, healer, dancer, and singer. Hailing from Hoonah, Alaska, of Tlingit, Cherokee, and Filipino descent, Gene works for the Native Wellness Institute as a deeply charismatic performer traveling around the world to share his culture.

I had a dream about Gene before I ever met him in person. In the dream, we were performing a very important ceremony together that involved carving a cedar plank and putting it in a freshwater stream that led to the ocean. Spurred by my dream, I tracked Gene down and shared the dream with him. In return, Gene shared a traditional story he knew about putting planks into the ocean as a powerful form of magic that you had to be careful with. This strange conversation and circumstance sparked a friendship with Gene, who soon became a regular guest teacher at the Anake program.

At a later date, I taught with Gene on the Tulalip reservation with a group of Native youth mentors. It was quite the day. I was the only white person involved with the group that day, and I shared teachings about bird language, animal forms, and natural movement with the group of leaders. I also watched Gene work his own storytelling, singing, mentoring, and healing magic with the group, helping the leaders open up and come alive with their own stories. We were holding matching and complementary primal skills.

When Gene introduces himself, like many of the Native teachers I've worked with, part of his introduction is the story of his ancestry and where he's from. He shares his Tlingit name, Guy Yaaw, and mentions that he's from the T'akdeintaan Clan, the Raven Freshwater Sockeye Clan from Hoonah, Alaska, and the child of Wooshketaan, Eagle Thunderbird Clan in Juneau, Alaska. Gene focuses on helping people share their story—not just who they think they are and what they do, but where they are from and who they *really* are as human beings. This includes discovering the ancient primal stories of where their ancestors came from and how they got here. Often in Native communities, history, ancestry, and the story of where we come from is a core part of what it means to be human. Acknowledging our primal, ancestral roots is how people introduce themselves.

"People don't know how to introduce themselves," he said. "They introduce themselves as what they do. Start learning about who you are as a human being. Reindigenize yourself, and find your deep nature connections. This adds to who you are and what you do—all that is healing. The more you find out about who you are and your connection to this world and nature, the more your ancestral DNA wakes up, and your ancestral wisdom wakes up."

So, in essence, become aware of our own ancestral, primal lineage.

Over the years, as the topics of cultural appropriation, decolonization, and power and privilege came up, Gene helped train and develop the staff's capacity to intelligently and compassionately look at these topics and also face some of the difficult facts about this country's history. Gene was a tremendous resource for me, the leadership team at WAS, and our other staff and students around these topics.

"I prefer the term *reindigenization* to decolonization," Gene said. "Reindigenization is getting back to nature connection, your ancestral skills. It's going back to those things, where you came from. As opposed to decolonizing, you are moving away from things, away from a different way of considering things. Reindigenizing is stepping back to something that's already waiting. Reindigenization and deep nature connection, survival skills are the same . . . It's a state of mind and a state of mind that starts by stepping back into the forest."

Consider it this way, from Gene's perspective. "When you step off the trail into the forest, you step into the threshold of spirit. Forest, mountain, and rivers are all spirit, as I was raised. Everything is just watching, and they are waiting. They say to you, 'We've been waiting for you.'"

This perspective is one of the core aspects of our primal journey: developing deep relationships with the nonhuman world, including plants, animals, trees, and even "inanimate" objects such as mountains and rivers.

Many of the Native teachers I've worked with, including Tony Ten Fingers, Gene Tagaban, and Gilbert Walking Bull, often talked in very spiritual terms. They would link events in nature as manifestations of spirit in action, and they encouraged others to watch for these things. For them, this was an important part of deep nature connection. It was part of the primal journey to learn and watch nature as a reflection of where we were on our path and to look to nature as a place for answers to our deepest questions.

During my interview with Gene for this book, a humming-bird flew up to me as we were having our conversation. It came quite close, almost landing on me, and its jeweled wings and throat glimmered in the sun.

"That's spirit talking, Nate," Gene commented. "Communication is happening all the time. Pay attention to it! Humming-bird—that's a sign that we're on the right path, that we're doing a good thing."

So how does Gene really feel about reindigenization, and what's his take on the greater survival skills and deep nature connection movement being filled with an awful lot of white folks?

For Gene, it was really quite simple. First of all, due to natural population demographics, there are a lot more white people in North America now, so, naturally, more of them will be involved in survival skills and deep nature connection. But Gene also suggested that non-Native people are less connected to their heritage due to migration and immigration and the influence of European settlers, and they are looking to re-establish their connection. And for Gene, these connections found in nature do belong to everybody. He sees them as universal truths:

"The earth doesn't care if you're white, black, Asian, or native. It doesn't care if you're Mouse or Bear or Deer or Slug. It takes you no matter who you are. There are universal truths out there, and they aren't connected to a specific tribe or heritage or people."

These universal truths might include the survival skills of making fire, creating stone tools, or learning to build a drum, and they don't belong to any one particular group. Bird language, collecting wild foods, watching for predators in our surroundings—these are all part of the core human experience and longing. Nature can be a teacher and source of inspiration for all of us.

But our ancient human primal nature also longs for more than just skills. Our relationship to others and the culture we carry is just as important. Native teachers have helped remind me of the importance of other intangibles, such as culture, inner work, and an appreciation of the sacred.

"One of my teachers told me, 'To connect with your inner nature, you must first connect with nature.' A healing path begins with knowing who we are and discovering our inner nature," shared Gene.

Gene's singing, dancing, storytelling, and mentoring are all forms of healing and his own primal work. This healing is a big part of what Gene shares in the Native community, whether it's with the Native Wellness Institute, the Nisqually Tribe, men's groups in Alaska, or suicide prevention work. One particular woman Gene worked with had exhibited a lot of unpredictable and even dangerous behaviors, occasionally erupting with bouts of aggression and intense anger. This young woman had an intense history of all kinds of abuse, and the staff who worked with her were at a loss for how to help her.

Gene didn't hesitate to implement what he thought would be most helpful for her: time outside in nature. Against the recommendations of staff and advisers, Gene took the woman outside to a nearby water area. Gene simply told her she was among her ancestors with the trees and river, and he sang songs while she said or did whatever she needed to do in that setting. This form of "treatment" was done repeatedly, and the patient even started to request it. Gene's nature treatment was instrumental in changing her behavior. Nature heals.

Gene's stories of healing and water reminded me of my own experiences. For years, I've sat on the banks of the Tolt River near my house in Washington. It's my core area to practice deep nature connection, listen to bird language, and practice my primal skills. I've been lucky enough to watch the salmon return year after year and see eagles and osprey fish nearby. Sometimes I've even found mink or elk tracks on the sandy beach. In addition to all of these deep nature experiences, that place has been a solace for me through some very hard times. Long before I heard Gene's take on nature treatments, I would dunk myself in the river to emerge refreshed, renewed, and with a different perspective. Nature as a healing force or source for people is an ancient human practice and probably one of the earliest forms of therapy we had as humans. Our primal selves seem to find spontaneous healing and renewal when given time in nature at a beautiful spot.

Gene uses nature not only to heal others, but to heal himself. When Gene was 29 going on 30, he hit a rough patch in his life. He decided to go on a big wander through Alaska, his own "big backyard," as he put it. He traveled throughout all of Alaska on a personal healing journey. Along the way, he did work-exchange programs and spent time in many different towns and villages. When he could, he fished and ate the food from the land and slept and stayed with Native people. He watched birds and ducks diving into the water, even as winter was setting in, and saw the deep strength and resilience of the people and the land. This was a balm for his wounds.

Toward the end of his wandering, Gene wound up in Anchorage. Very quickly, the toxicity and negativity of being in that city overwhelmed him. He fled back into nature nearby and sat on a beach near the ocean. Lots of emotions came up for him, and he felt the urge to look at a tall, majestic mountain behind him. Something inside him told him he needed to be on top of that mountain. So, he just ran up. Bare-chested, in his shorts, and with no water he ran up the mountain in a few hours.

At the top of the mountain, Gene allowed the birds, wind, rocks, and sun to cleanse him as he stood on a rocky precipice. He stayed there for a while, once again feeling that deep connection he had once lost.

"It really felt like Creation was letting me know I was going to be okay," he reflected.

When I heard this story from Gene it made me wonder how many other times have we as humans run to the tops of mountains to be healed inside? How old is this practice? Is this one of our original forms of primal healing?

~

Stories of Cannibal Giants are a well-known element of oral traditions for many Native groups living in northern climates of North America. Sometimes called *Wendigo* or *Wetiko*, these giants come in and feed on the flesh of the people. Gene shared with me about these stories: In one village, the youngest of three brothers asks his uncles how to defeat the giants who are plaguing his people. He trains and follows their advice and is able to overcome the giants, but he does so in a disrespectful way. As a result, the giants come back to life in a much smaller form—as mosquitoes, beings that still feed on flesh and blood. The moral of the story is that those giants may not look like they used to, but they're still here today. Per Gene:

"Those Cannibal Giants are here today. They take the form of racism, hatred, anger and violence . . . they are still around, and we have to be careful not to feed them."

Several other authors and Native experts share this perspective. Jack D. Forbes, a Native American scholar, writer, and political activist who was involved in the early days of the American Indian Movement and helped found the first Native American college not located on a reservation, was known for many things. But one of his books—*Columbus and Other Cannibals*—has been instrumental as a critique of Western civilization and is listed as a major influence by many involved in anti-civilization and decolonization work. Forbes puts forth the idea that modern humans suffer from a disease, an illness that affects our minds, and which is encompassed by the term *wetiko* in the Native Cree language or *wendigo* in Native Ojibwa language. These terms originally referred to a form of extreme greed or gluttony that could cause a person to become possessed and transform into a Cannibal Giant, like Gene referred to.

Forbes put forth the argument that modern society, especially our materialistic, war-driven society, suffers from a collective form of this *wetiko* disorder. His ideas have influenced others, such as Derrick Jensen, a well-known eco-anarchist writer, who have taken Forbes's ideas and applied them to our most recent political, economic, and psychological activities. In his book, *Dispelling Wetiko: Breaking the Curse of Evil*, Paul Levy posits that we all need to figure out a way to rid ourselves of this "mind-virus."

It's hard to say what is really going on; the complexities of decolonization, cultural appropriation, history, and communication often make things challenging between Native and non-Native people. Over time, perhaps we can all slowly work toward resolving these things and even toward the greater goal of reconciliation. My experience has shown that survival skills, deep nature connection, and exploring our primal roots helps us discover our core humanity and what unites us as humans, not what separates and divides us.

Sherri Mitchell, a very powerful and eloquent Native teacher, activist, and leader from the Penobscot Indian reservation, is diving into that work now. She has worked for 25 years with environmental justice and Indigenous rights groups across North America, using her background as a lawyer to protect land and water rights and preserve indigenous ways of life. Specifically, Sherri works to support the position of the Wabanaki people of northeast North America. The Wabanaki were the people of first contact with European settlers, explorers, and colonizers and also suffered the first rounds of wounds and betrayal.

Recently, Sherri has been the visionary behind a new ceremony aiming to heal some of these deep wounds and heal the disconnect between all humans, their relationship with each other, and with the Creation. The ceremony she helped design is called "Healing the Wounds of Turtle Island" (Turtle Island being a Native name for North America), which will take place over the next *21 years*. The ceremony is open to everyone and has been attended by people from all over the world, including all continents except Antarctica.

Sherri openly speaks of this ceremony as being a fulfillment of prophecy passed down by her ancestors. It is designed to start in the "Eastern Door," the eastern part of North America where contact first happened, and it will stay there for 4 years, and then begin a journey to different sites in the cardinal directions, spending 4 years at each site. The ceremony will culminate in the 21st year by returning to the east for its closing.

Ceremonies like the one Sherri formed function to work on reconciliation, decolonization, and our primal longings for deep connection to the land we all now call home. Work like this may be vital for all of us to navigate these issues going forward.

⸻

While there are no easy answers around these complicated issues, it seems that the work of reconciliation can take many forms. Almost a decade ago, my 4-year-old daughter, Katie, and I were invited by a friend to come to a gathering of the Samish tribe on their traditional lands on Samish Island in the northern part of the Salish Sea.

Dr. Randall Eaton, who my friend knew, had gotten permission to spend time with the Samish elders recording and learning about their experiences with orca whales. I had been invited as a special guest to share my own stories of encounters with orcas to the elders, along with a few other non-tribal members. It was very last-minute on a weekend in late summer, and I had to gather everything very quickly to go up for the day. On a whim as we were about to leave, I threw in some apples from my yard to bring as a gift, and I also collected some special bow-drill materials I had laying around.

The drive was beautiful on the way up, heading along the highway as we moved ever closer to the waters of the Puget Sound. The majesty of the Cascade Mountains was on our right to the east, and the Olympic Mountains were off to our left and the west. There was hardly any snow left on the mountains, but they were still beautiful, framing our drive and eloquently reminding us that we live in a land of mountains and sea.

When we got to the location for the gathering, I was a little surprised to find that the event was actually happening at an old Campfire Boys and Girls camp. It turns out that a lot of camps are located at culturally significant spots, and so the Samish had permission to use this site for their own annual family camp, which we were about to walk into.

Soon after we arrived, a circle gathering opened the day, and people sang songs, played drums, and formed a circle of gratitude, sharing something we were thankful for. I was struck immediately by how familiar everything felt, and Katie was quick to pull me aside and mention, "Daddy, I feel like we're at WAS."

After the opening circle, there was some craft time, and Katie made beaded necklaces with the other kids. I managed to track someone down from the kitchen to share our apples, and I received a big smile and warm thanks for contributing some food from my own yard for the day. Soon, another craft session broke out, and I found myself sitting across from a Samish woman around my own age. She was making cordage—a form of natural rope—out of plant fibers from nettle and dogbane. We swapped techniques of how to make cordage from lap-rolling, which I'd learned at ALI, to the reverse-wrap technique, which was popular at WAS and the Tracker School.

After a session where the kids played games together, a time followed for people to pursue their own interests. Katie and I decided to wander over to the fire pit to play with my bow-drill kit. I've mentioned before that fire kits can be very fickle, but that day the fire gods were surely smiling down on me, as I was able to crank out coal after coal with ease. As soon as some of the first smoke came out of my kit, a group of kids ran over and watched as I used the bow-drill to create a coal. After that first coal came to life, I flipped it into a cedar bundle and allowed Katie and all of the other kids to blow on it to bring it to life. They were so excited, and their faces lit up with wonder as the tinder burst into flame again and again. In fact, I had to keep putting out my tinder bundle and reusing it because there was so much excitement around making more coals.

Soon, a father and son—Joseph and Matthias—joined our circle, and they were very focused and intent on what I was doing. Having seen the look on the dad's face before, I knew what my next step was.

"Want to give it a try?" I asked Joseph.

His eyes lit up with excitement, and, with just a little coaching, Joseph had smoke pouring out of the kit. Within about 20 minutes, he had his first coal and was blowing into life his first tinder bundle with the help of his son. Needless to say, our fire-making attracted a fair bit of attention from the camp, including the elders shooting curious glances our way.

The father and son duo hung around with me quite a bit as we got ready for lunch, and Joseph kept asking me questions about what kind of wood to use and how to make your own kit. I shared with him what I could, and it felt like something unexpected was happening. I thought I had come to Samish Island to share an orca story with the elders, and now some sort of other exchange was occurring.

After lunch, where my apples were offered as part of the meal, Randall set everything up at the beach to film the elders and have everyone share their stories—the reason why I came for the day. The wind was blowing and gray clouds moved in over the water. Huge piles of massive driftwood formed a natural little amphitheater where we all sat. The elders, dressed in traditional regalia, sat and listened stoically to the stories, including mine about the orca whales.

As Katie and I gathered our things for the 3-hour drive back home, Joseph and Matthias approached us to say goodbye. They were filled with energy and had perma-grins on their face. As Joseph asked me a few more questions about how to make a kit and where to find the wood, I realized why I was there that day.

I looked him in the eye, thanked him for his earnestness and enthusiasm around fire-making, and then handed him the kit.

"I think you should take this. It belongs here now. Take it as a gift, and thanks for all the hospitality and generosity that we've been shown today."

Joseph's eyes lit up.

As I drove home, Katie quickly fell asleep in her car seat in the back of my car. The sun broke through the clouds, and the sky lit up with mixed colors. The light reflected off the waters of Puget Sound, and the distant mountains made everything soft, warm, and luminous. Soon after leaving the Samish camp, I saw two herons and, once I made it back to the main highway, I spotted a coyote running through a farmer's field. And then suddenly a thought crashed into my consciousness. To this day I'm not sure it's totally true—but, I'm pretty sure that friction fire-making had died out among the Samish. Somehow, fate had arranged for something special to happen that day. And now, with a lightning-kissed fire kit made from a shard of cedar wood, ancient fire-making had been reintroduced in a totally magical way.

Decolonization, reindigenization, and reconciliation are very complicated topics to explore and unpack, but, for one day at least, it all made sense and felt good. Primal skills and our journey toward our primal nature can be what unites us, not divides us.

CHAPTER 7

Primal Origins: Out of Africa and Toward Wakanda

Wakanda will no longer watch from the shadows. We cannot. We must not. We will work to be an example of how we as brothers and sisters on this earth should treat each other. Now, more than ever, the illusions of division threaten our very existence. We all know the truth: more connects us than divides us. But in times of crisis, the wise build bridges, while the foolish build barriers. We must find a way to look after one another as if we were one single tribe.

—T'CHALLA, KING OF WAKANDA, PORTRAYED BY
CHADWICK BOSEMAN IN THE MOVIE *BLACK PANTHER*

AS PEOPLE EXPLORE THEIR HUNTER-GATHERER NATURE AND unlock their primal longings and needs, they often become curious about human origins. I've definitely followed this curiosity time and time again, and while I love exploring the ideas presented in this book with people and places around the world, there is one place that all of these paths lead: our continent of origin—Africa. This is one of the reasons why so many teachers in this movement have gone back to study with the Bushmen or have done extensive tracking immersion classes in the heart of African wild lands.

Primal humanity arose in Africa, and if we take our roots back far enough, Africa is where we find ourselves.

Of course this produces a lot of interesting questions and conundrums for a movement that, until recently, has been made up of mostly white folks. We'd be remiss if, when talking about the primal movement, we did not touch upon how one's race affects participation in the movement. This is an increasingly relevant topic, as our society faces racial challenges on a daily basis, and topics like privilege and power need to be discussed more now than ever before.

In my discussion with Gene Tagaban about the battles we have with the modern-day "Cannibal-Giant" of racism and prejudice, Gene shared another traditional story about these very issues.

As the story of the "Battle with the North Wind" goes, a young man was shunned by his village for the color of his skin. His skin was the color of soot because he had been too close to the fire. The young man was excluded from his people and experienced prejudice and shame due to his appearance. However, this young man was determined to prove his worth, and so he would train at night when everyone else was asleep. He jumped in cold water and whipped himself with spruce and cedar boughs to toughen his skin and body. He climbed trees, lifted rocks, and engaged in his own unique form of Earthgym and natural movement, all in seeking to prove his worth to his people. Eventually, the Spirit of the North Wind (a personification of cold, ice, and the challenge of winter) noticed his efforts, and offered to challenge him in a wrestling match. The North Wind promised that, if the soot-skinned young man won, he would be strong enough to lead his people. They battled back and forth, with the young man finally winning and defeating the North Wind. This young man went on to become a great leader for his people.

I'd heard other variations of this "Battle with the North Wind" story before, but never one where the main hero had skin the color of soot who suffered prejudice and rejection from his own people. This story reminded me of the challenges of teaching and bringing survival skills to people of all walks of life from all backgrounds.

What happens when these teachings of deep nature connection, our primal nature, and survival skills are offered to kids who have never really been off pavement in their life? How do you navigate the dynamics of primarily white teachers offering this kind of experience to a group of all African-American students? Do these teachings really work for everybody? What if you associate being barefoot or dirty or going off trail with traumas that happened to your family or ancestors just a few generations ago?

Conjuring up these questions reminds me of a program I helped run several years ago. A Montessori-inspired public school from the south side of Seattle approached WAS to do a multiday event with their kids at a residential camp in the forest of the foothills of the Cascade Mountains. The school was full of kids who had never been out of the city, and the population of students was predominantly African-American. They had worked with WAS 5 years earlier, and they were excited to do something again, appreciating a similarity of approach in helping awaken a child's natural gifts, and a desire to have their students spend some quality time in nature.

I was the on-site director of the program, tasked with bringing over a hundred kids to the camp to be taught by nine apprentice instructors. We stood on the hillside of Camp River Ranch (the site we were partnering with) and watched busload after busload of kids arrive. The kids' faces reflected anxiety, excitement, wonder, and fear. The apprentice instructors, who had never taught this demographic of kids before, mirrored the same feelings in their own faces.

At one of our first meetings that evening over dinner, the apprentices were already a little overwhelmed and overwrought.

"The kids don't even want to step on the grass, let alone go in the forest," shared one apprentice, already facing a little bit of panic.

"Look, nobody said this was going to be easy," I consoled them. "But, I know deep down these kids love nature too—it's just newer to them. It's exciting and overwhelming, and it's probably just as fun for all of them to be in their cabins as it is to go into the woods. Let's focus on them feeling safe and oriented, and then see what happens."

The transformation came quickly. Just 3 days later, the kids were chasing each other through the woods and playing games where they crawled on their bellies in the bushes. They didn't need to sit on benches or stay on the concrete road through the camp. They were alive, excited, and enjoying pretending to be wild animals, making fire, or learning about the differences in the many trees all around.

After the program ended, and after the students had enthusiastically—and some sadly—waved goodbye to us from the buses, the apprentices and I sat in a circle and shared highlights and lessons from the field trip. For many, this had been one of the hardest programs they had ever taught, but at the same time it was also one of the most rewarding. The changes in the kids after 3 days were palpable and very apparent. Most of the children had gone from being scared of being pushed out of their comfort zone to feeling like the forest, rocks, rivers, and lake could be a safe, fun place to play—and all within a few days.

There is a pretty valid criticism that a lot of the deep nature connection work and the primal movement in general has mostly been for white people from relatively privileged backgrounds. However, that is changing. Just like in the broader context of people of color spending time in nature or participating in outdoor sports, such as rock climbing, skiing, hiking, camping, and backpacking, more and more people of color and people from diverse backgrounds are exploring their own experience of deep nature connection, survival, and time immersed in nature. Over the years,

I have seen increased diversity at both the youth and adult level, locally in Washington State, and across the world as I have traveled and taught. There are more and more adults and children of color in all of these kinds of programs, as well as a healthy dose of diversity around gender and sexual identity.

These groups of people bring their own unique backgrounds, histories, and wonderful questions, inquiries, and ideas to the primal movement. In particular, they often provide thought-provoking questions around power and privilege, and have brought forth the important emphasis that nature itself is hugely diverse and that diversity is an asset that brings resiliency, flexibility, adaptability, and creativity in the animal, plant, and human worlds.

It is probably not a surprise to most people that most (though not all) of the instructors and teachers in this field are white. It may be surprising to some folks, however, that a large swath of these teachers are women, and that the overall demographic is starting to swing toward more people of color, as well as an increase in people who identify as transgender or people for whom traditional gender categories don't work.

Ironically, Wilderness Awareness School was started by two white guys, both of whom were carrying powerful potent lineages from nonwhite people: Jon Young and Ingwe. This is inherently problematic and troublesome for some people, including some of the instructors carrying on those lineages today. Jon Young carried on the teachings he received from Tom Brown Jr. that included specific Apache teachings and practices around tracking, survival, deep nature connection, and awareness when he met Ingwe (aka Norman Powell) in an organic restaurant over 30 years ago. Ingwe was carrying similar specific practices from his own experiences with Akamba, Zulu, and San Bushmen tribal groups.

I can only imagine the conversation that the two of them had that day that led to the birth of what would become Wilderness Awareness School and eventually 8 Shields and the global deep nature connection movement. One of the things that struck both

Ingwe and Jon was the overlap and similarity of what they had learned in widely different contexts. Essentially, the Apache scout tradition Jon had learned in New Jersey from Tom Brown Jr., at its core, was very similar to what Ingwe had learned within the very different landscapes and cultural traditions of Kenya and other parts of Africa.

Ingwe's story only adds levels of irony and complexity to the situation. Norman Powell was born to white settlers (who some might refer to colonizers) in South Africa, and later his family moved to Kenya. When he was a child, his parents hired a local older boy from the Akamba tribe, named Ndaka, to care and watch for Norman and keep him out of trouble. Ndaka and Norman became close friends. Ndaka introduced Norman to the traditional native skills of the Akamba tribe. As Norman grew up in Kenya, he ended up becoming close with several African tribes, receiving the honorific Ingwe or "leopard" as his name. As he grew older, Ingwe shared these traditional skills with African youth, including helping found the African branch of the Boy Scouts (which, coincidentally, had been started by Ingwe's uncle, Baden Powell). The scouts kept alive traditional survival skills, bushcraft, and nature connection practices for different tribal groups. Later, Ingwe and his wife, Elizabeth, moved to New Jersey, where Ingwe, as one of its co-founders, became a grandfather figure for WAS.

The central fire and the Akamba-style hut at the heart of the land of Wilderness Awareness School is named Malalo ya Chui, the Lair of the Leopard, in honor of Ingwe. Ingwe passed away in 2005, and Elizabeth came to WAS for an honoring. Ingwe's ashes were scattered around the outside of Malalo and in the fire pit. To this day, his entire nature museum, including tribal garb, a leopard skin, and his spear, adorn the wall of Cedar Lodge, a teaching classroom at WAS.

I remember two main primal lessons from time spent with Ingwe. One was an awareness exercise that was essential if you were spending time in the African bush. Dubbed the "Leopard

Walk," the exercise essentially has you pause after ten slow steps taken in a natural setting (forest, mountain, desert, or jungle). At each pause, you listen, look around, and look behind you and above you. While it's easy to assume that you are moving like a leopard, in actuality you are moving slowly and cautiously checking out your surroundings for danger, including leopards. One of their favorite ways to catch prey is to stalk them from behind or drop on them from above. (The walk is named Leopard Walk to make sure you are not being stalked by a leopard.) But the Leopard Walk is applicable in plenty of settings outside of Africa. Not getting eaten by leopards is indeed an important primal survival skill!

The other lesson passed down from Ingwe involved him discussing how to conduct oneself. He was known to frequently say, "Common sense is not so bloody common anymore!" He also chastised instructors, apprentices, and students when they showed up for events or in public with torn pants, dirty feet, or looking disheveled. For Ingwe, a core part of survival training and deep nature connection was being able to blend into any environment.

"You should be able to spend the whole day out in the bush, and then at the end of the day change your shirt, splash some fresh water on your face, and walk into a dinner party eloquently mingling with the guests," he would say.

This theme of what he called "walking in two worlds" was a core part of what he taught, and a valuable lesson for all of us as we navigate the perplexing paradox of our ancient primal side and the modern world.

While Ingwe's story, passing, and legacy are quite powerful stories, what is it like for actual people of color, and, in particular, African-American people to sit in Cedar Lodge with pictures of a white man in Africa on the wall? What is it like to spend time around a fire in an African-style hut built by white people? And what is it like to participate in a program called the Anake Outdoor School, a program named after the term *Anake*, an Akamba word that means protector?

There is no one answer to the above questions, but I've made it a point to try to connect with people of color over the years about their experiences in the programs. What are the ups and downs? What works and what doesn't?

Many of the people of color I've talked to have found that their time participating in programs at WAS, whether it's at the year-long program of Anake, only for a weekend workshop, or having their kids in a day camp, has been very powerful and positive because of the deep nature connection and survival skills shared. Yet there is also a lot of complexity, confusion, and sometimes even hurt around the difficulties about cultural appropriation.

Multiple African-American men who went through Anake have told me very directly that they never felt so welcome, understood, and seen as they did when they were in the program. They also resonated deeply with the emphasis on universal core nature connection practices from around the world.

Some of those same men say that a deep reflection around sharing names, stories, songs, and lineage would be really helpful, given the complex dynamics involving power, history, and current events that revolve around black and white relations in the United States.

Jackie Warren is the first ever African-American female graduate from the Anake program. Jackie has had a fascinating life both as a nuclear safety inspector and as a world traveler. She has faced racism in many forms during her travels in different parts of the world, in some cases because she was the first black person or black woman anybody had seen. She was drawn to come to the Anake program in 2016, needing a break from the world of nuclear inspection, and seeking something that resonated with her larger worldview and experiences.

During Jackie's time as a student and afterward, I kept a dialogue with her about her experiences, both positive and negative, in the program. She appreciated that there was a day every fall that focused on power, privilege, and racial dynamics to set context for the program for everyone. Yet, it was still hard for her fellow students to really understand her experience of what it was like to be a black woman in the program or even living in the area.

Jackie shared with me that, while she didn't necessarily experience direct racism from her fellow students in the program, she certainly experienced some explicit and appalling racist behavior outside of the program in the surrounding areas. At the job Jackie worked during her time at Anake, she was passed over numerous times for a promotion, even though she had been promised one by her supervisor. Not surprising to Jackie, those who were promoted were attractive white people, often younger candidates who had spent less time at the job than her. These issues eventually led to Jackie quitting her job while in the Anake program, and having to live very tightly to make it all the way until the end of the program. A large number of her fellow white students did not need to work during the program, as they received financial help during the program from a family member to pay their tuition and housing.

Jackie also shared other stories of her differences with some of her classmates, like how the white female students never could get why she didn't want to get her hair wet. Later, Jackie shared a chilling story with me. Several of her friends from the program were excited to go to the city on an adventure. They wanted to go to Seattle and test their "scout skills" out in an urban environment. Their goal was to move around with stealth and urban camouflage, and practice being unseen in an environment way different than the mossy forest they were used to. When Jackie was invited to participate, she politely but firmly declined.

Jackie didn't have the heart to share directly with them that you don't just go sneaking around a city as a black person; it's inherently dangerous, and you might get shot by the police. These kinds of conversations with Jackie reminded me of some time I got to spend with Dr. Caprice Hollins, an African-American woman who co-founded Cultures Connecting with her business partner,

Ilsa Govan. Cultures Connecting is a premier, cutting-edge organization that provides much of the diversity training around race for businesses and organizations in the Puget Sound area. I attended a few of their trainings in conjunction with WAS's newly formed after school programs for diverse kids in the south part of Seattle. I was able to invite Dr. Hollins out to WAS to help train the entire staff to broaden their cultural awareness and be better equipped to work with a wider audience.

The day we spent with Dr. Hollins was truly amazing and eye-opening. She took us through a series of exercises, games, and stories that illustrated hidden gaps in our awareness, particularly related to race. It was a whole new level of awareness for the Wilderness Awareness School. But there were a few things Dr. Hollins saved for the end of the day that really stuck with me.

"I just want to share something with all of you, now that we have some trust from our day together," she began. "This man over here is barefoot. And that makes me uncomfortable . . . it might seem like a strange thing for me to say, but it does. I want to let you know why."

Dr. Hollins explained how, from her perspective, it was quite ironic that one of the core things we were doing was helping people be barefoot or get dirty as a way of connecting to nature. While she easily related to the idea of recycling or hiking as environmental actions, deliberately putting mud on one's face or clothes or crawling through the bushes had too many associations with the historical trauma of slavery and also poverty.

"Black people dress nice for a reason. We can't get away with 'being dirty' for being dirty's sake. For too long, being barefoot meant being poor and not being able to afford shoes."

At the end of the day, Dr. Hollins encouraged us all to read the book *Post-Traumatic Slavery Disorder*. She thought it would give us a lot of insight into why black students might not be so interested or willing to easily participate in some of the activities we were running for adults and kids.

Diversity and Depth

The field of deep nature connection, survival skills, and even youth rites of passage work is undergoing tremendous change as the schools and instructors are diversifying their staff, messaging, and who they serve. Darcy Ottey, who has worked extensively with Journeys Rites of Passage and Youth Passageways, has been one of the leading voices in the field looking at power and privilege dynamics in this work. Queer Nature was founded by Pinar and So, two nonbinary folks who also go by Creature and Faun. Their program has been wildly successful at reaching out to the LBGT+ communities. Wilderness Youth Project in Santa Barbara, California, has taken diverse and underprivileged youth on epic nature adventures for years. Wilderness Torah has formed to look at the intricacies and connection between deep nature connection work and Judaism. Finally, Victor Wooten, a prominent African-American singer, songwriter, bassist, and performer who has studied at the Tracker School and with Jon Young, has run Bass and Nature Camp for years, bringing together youth from all backgrounds to immerse themselves in the study of nature, survival skills, and music for weeks at a time.

Carter McBride, an African-American man in his 60s, is a recent Anake grad, and also a member of the relatively new Equity Council formed in 2018 at WAS. Carter's background is in both the Boy Scouts of America and the National Outdoor Leadership School (NOLS). At NOLS, he has held many different roles, from student to instructor to diversity and inclusion mentor and eventually serving as an advisor to their Board of Trustees on the topic of diversity and inclusion. Carter's love affair with the primal movement and nature formed in the Wind River Range in Wyoming, where he was struck with awe at the epic beauty of nature, realizing that he wanted to spend the rest of his life connecting with nature after a full career in corporate sales in the pharmaceutical industry.

I asked Carter to describe his approach to this work:

"I'm an innate believer in all possibilities in both professional and personal growth, especially in outdoor experiential learning with emphasis in increased active multiracial/multicultural inclusiveness."

Doing this work is something that Carter loves deeply. It oozes out in his expression, his animated sharing, and in his lively vitality for someone in his 60s still quite active in a field that tends to be dominated by people in their 20s and 30s. Carter recalled at his NOLS leadership training course how he was, by far, the eldest of his group. The next youngest person was 28. However, he was able to keep up—it just took him a lot longer to recover after each day.

This wild drive and fortitude came out when I asked Carter about some of his favorite times at Anake. One of the best times he had was when he joined a choice-based group for a week one winter. The group was focusing on developing endurance, cold-training, and physical capacity. The small group was led by Kyle, one of the Anake instructors in his late 20s who specializes in training in cold-water immersion, parkour, and pushing the limits of human possibility. Again, Carter was by far the oldest of the group, but he seemed to have no trouble jumping into the ice-cold water in the middle of January with the temperature just above freezing. A different form of primal awareness and training for sure! Carter and his crew spent 3 days doing cold-training, running around the woods, and jumping over logs and crawling through the mud.

The experience culminated for all of them when they had to move through the pond blindfolded to reach the other side and then build a fire out of hemlock on the opposite shore. The experience was an ultimate bonding for Carter with his fellow classmates. Simply breathing the air after these kinds of experiences made it feel so pure, "almost like a drug."

It's funny how Carter ended up at Anake. It was not a linear path, and was quite unexpected. After his successful corporate career, Carter was looking for something that would take him beyond what he called, "the perceptions of success." Having checked off the societal norms of what defines success, what else was there? For him, the answer seemed related to nature and survival, but he did not expect to end up in a survival immersion program.

The summer before Carter joined Anake, he and his wife were asked to help watch his grandchildren for a couple of weeks while his stepson taught at a program. He was needed to watch the kids at a Stone Age gathering called Saskatoon Circle, which took place in central Washington. Even after all of his training at NOLS, Carter was still struck by how much there was to learn about nature and the wild, primal human experience.

During his week at Saskatoon, Carter focused on animal butchering and processing and learned to graciously give death to animals, and then how to use all of the parts of the animal in a way that honored its sacrifice. Having grown up in Oklahoma City learning to grill, smoke, and barbecue meat, the experience opened him up to a whole other level of relationship to food. It was at this program where Carter met a recent Anake grad and became intrigued about the idea of joining a program where you did activities like that all the time.

Carter set out to see if Anake was a right fit for him, despite some of his mentors hesitating. But Carter had a conversation with one person he trusted and had seen grads from the program before.

"You know Nate, he told me what he'd seen. He'd seen grads from other programs, from more typical outdoor education and environmental programs. The Anake grads had more resiliency, more capacity."

This was the kind of thing Carter was looking for, and he joined the program.

But, what kinds of things did Carter experience around power, privilege, and racial dynamics? What were the challenges that he experienced at WAS, and how did that parallel his experience with other groups like NOLS?

It boiled down to some very specific things, especially having a conversation with those that do not look like you, to paraphrase Carter. And, during those conversations, being willing to look at concepts such as avoidance, acknowledgment, cultural appropriation, egos, history, acceptance, openness to change, and so on. These core issues get to the heart of the challenges we face around race, power, and privilege everywhere.

These issues have not just been a part of Carter's life because he was a black man growing up in the American Midwest and then working in the corporate world for many years. He literally grew up as a child at the knees of civil rights leaders. His uncle was Jimmy Stewart, who played a prominent role in bringing successful racial change to Oklahoma. Carter remembers his grandmother cooking breakfast, lunch, and dinner for people like Martin Luther King Jr., Thurgood Marshall, and Ralph Ellison.

What intersection does Carter see between his background growing up with civil rights leaders and his current work in the field of nature connection, survival, and outdoor education? How do people of color relate to this whole idea of connecting with their primal selves?

Carter answered this question by sharing part of the story of Malcolm X with me. He pointed out that there's a very specific section in Malcolm's autobiography where he describes being given a small piece of ground to make a garden and grow peas. It suggests that even this famous civil rights leader experienced his own moments of nature connection. This is listed as one of the happier times in Malcolm's life, and he specifically describes finding peace after gardening in *The Autobiography of Malcolm X*:

"And sometimes when I had everything straight and clean for my things to grow, I would lay down on my back between two rows and I would gaze up in the blue sky at the clouds moving and thinking all kinds of things."

Carter also shared with me a quote from J. Drew Lanham (an African-American wildlife professor at Clemson University and board member with Audubon South Carolina and the American Birding Association):

"The wild things and places belong to all of us. So, while I can't fix the bigger problems of race in the United States and World, I can prescribe a solution in my own small corner. Get more People of Color out there. Turn oddities into commonplace. Our responsibility is to pass something on to those coming after."

Conversations with Jackie, Carter, and others like them can definitely shed some light on how the experience of primal activities such as survival skills training or deep nature connection might be significantly different for people based on the historical context of their ethnic and racial identity. Carter, for instance, shared how he felt he had already honed his survival and awareness skills before ever knowing about Anake by having to carry large amounts of pharmaceuticals into dangerous neighborhoods. Getting in and out of those situations suggests an activation of innate primal awareness, as well as a reality different from a simulated survival situation. Similarly, my friend Andrew Ford, an African-American tracker and survival skills student, shared that one of his reasons for diving into the world of survival and primal skills was his fear of being homeless someday. If that happened, he wanted to be ready. Now that he's a successful real estate investor, his reasons for studying survival skills and tracking have shifted, but behind it all he still remembers that initial impulse. Mostly, he continues to pursue these things because of his love for them and his own primal awakening.

While these stories help to illuminate the African-American experience of the world of survival skills, deep nature connection, and related arts, I feel that there's still a lot for all of us to unlock about our true primal heritage and ancestral longings by going back further: to Africa itself.

It was not lost on those I interviewed for this chapter that there were serious ironies around Ingwe and his role at WAS. But, even more than that, a bigger truth, often forgotten, has been unveiled: *we're all from Africa.* That's right—all of us. This is not some secret conspiracy theory. It's Anthropology 101. The cradle of humanity is Africa. All of our ancestors are from there. In fact, there have been multiple waves at different times of human and pre-human primate ancestors that arose and then migrated from Africa. It doesn't get any more primal for all humans than Africa.

There are two very important widely accepted theories on this. The first is the "Out of Africa" hypothesis. This idea suggests that anatomically modern humans developed between 300,000 to 200,000 years ago in Africa and then migrated to the rest of the world. While there is evidence of interbreeding with existing other archaic human types in other parts of Africa and Europe, genetic studies in different populations have confirmed that humanity as a whole is descended from this migration and other subsequent migrations out of Africa.

Taking a slightly different lens on the same topic, the "Mito-chondrial Eve Hypothesis" has shown that, through mitochon-drial DNA studies, we are actually all descended from one single female lineage that converge in one woman in Africa around 150,000 years ago. This means we all have a great-grandmother to the nth degree in Africa somewhere. Paleoanthropologists have also added a "Y-Chromosomal Adam Hypothesis" showing that a similar process exists for our Y-chromosome DNA.

While subsequent DNA research has shown that we could all share a much more recent matrilineal ancestor (common ancient grandmother), it does not dispute the basic premise that we are all descended both through a female line and a male line from ancient African sources.

But, what does this mean, and why is it important? How does this play out in our primal longings and our underlying hunter-gatherer instincts?

It may be that on a deep level—perhaps even a neurological one—we expect to look at an African landscape. It is a quite common point of view in the field of anthropology that we unconsciously groom our landscapes around us to look like the African savannah. How is this possible, and what is the evidence? Look no further than your lawn and the parks we build. Our desire to have open space filled with grass, interspersed with some trees as our ideal play and relaxation area, is supposedly us making the land around us look like the ancient ancestral African savannah that the earliest humans called home.

People describe their experiences going to different parts of Africa—in particular, to experience encounters with large African wildlife in natural habitat—as some deep ancestral knowing and longing that had been met. Similarly, people who've had a chance to participate in African dance around a fire lasting late into the night echoed these same sentiments. And isn't it odd how we make sure our children (no matter where we are located geographically) are intimately acquainted from an early age with African animals, such as lions, hippos, giraffes, rhinos, hyenas, leopards, cheetahs, monkeys, and gorillas? We do this even though their chance of encountering these animals in any setting other than a zoo is very slim. In fact, a lot of children are more familiar with Africa's fauna than the animals that live in their own bioregion.

To understand this primal and epic longing for Africa, I approached author and self-described Afro-futurist, Steven Barnes. Barnes is an African-American science fiction writer and speaker whose popular works have crossed multiple genres and explore themes of our distant past, our current lives, and speculating at possible futures. In his work, the theme of our wild, primal ancestral selves lies just beneath the surface waiting to break out and take over through the thin veneer of civilization. Often, his characters have complex racial identities with some connection to the magic or potency of ancestral Africa. In his novels, black and white characters can be both heroes and villains, and sometimes the wild, primal energy beneath the surface can be unleashed both as a force for good or for evil.

One of Barnes's groundbreaking works was *Great Sky Woman*. This was, in many ways, a black author's response to the success of books like *Clan of the Cave Bear*. The story takes place in ancient Africa, at the base of Mount Kilimanjaro, and depicts a no-holds-barred look at ancient hunter-gatherer life in Africa, based on Steven's personal research into the topic (which included going on safari and being charged by elephants, his very own core primal experience!).

What was the inspiration behind this work, and why was it important?

"Well, I don't know if you've noticed this, Nate," Steven began, "but every museum diorama I've ever seen depicting cave-people has shown them as white. I think there's something missing."

Steven was quick to share that, in his mind, it was a positive sign that his publishing company and editors (run mostly by white folks) were the ones who suggested the idea and encouraged him to write the book and its sequel. This is also true with Steven's other work, including his very interesting take on an alternative American history called *Lion's Blood*. In this envisioned world, America is run by black Muslims of African origin, and white Europeans were forcibly removed from their homelands and turned into slaves. In *Lion's Blood* and its sequels, there are sympathetic and positive depictions of people in all the roles, both slave and master, as well as dark, twisted people on both sides. Many of the main characters struggle with a deep, aggressive, primal instinct boiling beneath the surface that can erupt and cause unbelievable violence to the world around them.

This is part of a big theme in Barnes's work and life (which you can check out at afrofuturist.com and stevenbarnes.com). Steven has studied martial arts for decades and trained with premier masters around the world. In our discussion, he didn't hesitate to bring up what he saw as the underlying contradictions he saw as our primal nature struggles in the face of a highly technological society. Studying martial arts, discovering our own relationship to aggression, fear, and struggle, and even watching combative entertainment, such as the mixed martial arts fights of the UFC, are all part of our underlying primal animal selves just below the surface.

"Our struggles with primal wildness are in part due to the demonization and mixed messages around archetypal male energies such as aggression. We want to move away from tooth and claw, but it's dangerous to forget how we got here," said Barnes.

Barnes sees society as programming men to be some sort of killer drone with dulled emotions and the inability to feel pain. He points out the normalization of male death in movies and the media as something that is regularly accepted, and that we are taught to not care about our emotions.

"It's as if we are trained to be brutes, then blamed for being brutish," he summarized. This creates a contradiction for those unlocking their primal instincts and underlying hunter-gatherer nature, as they receive many mixed messages about how to channel this energy and these impulses in a healthy way. This seems particularly true for men pursuing a primal path. How do they find an outlet for their primal, wild side without becoming destructive? This deeper, darker side of being primal can be hard to reconcile.

Barnes has made peace with this journey through his martial arts training. He's found a way to have that primal aggression alive and expressed, but his heart open and not shut down. Ultimately, this is one of the main goals of that kind of training: making peace with our primal wild instincts, but not shutting down our innate emotional awareness and capacity.

Steven sees the intellectual and technological world that we live in protecting us from some of these killer instincts. But we can't forget that all of our beauty and safety rests on top of survival and deep primal instincts that include the impulse to protect, defend, and possibly even kill. This is something we have needed to survive in the face of adversity over millennia.

"Survival short circuits everything," he shared. "And we have to feel safe in order to feel love."

The key is to find a balance of being in touch with these deep primal instincts, drives, and powers without losing our core humanity and emotional connection to others.

Why did Steven think it was so important to explore these themes in his work, and why does Africa feature so prominently as an archetypal image?

"Quite simply, African-Americans are the only people on the planet with no creation myth. Your chance of knowing your ancestry and tracing it back to a creation story is basically nil," he pointed out. There is a lack of a primal, primordial creation story and a void of cultural teachings and connection due to this disconnection from Africa.

Steven's written works and the classes he teaches repeatedly try to address this need for African-American people. His stories directly tried to fill this void. However, that void has changed somewhat recently. Several months before the movie *Black Panther* came to the screen, Steven predicted that this movie would be bigger than anyone was expecting. He had seen the reaction of audiences, especially black audiences, to just the movie trailer, and he accurately said that this would be a cultural moment for black people in America and for the whole world.

Black Panther grossed *$1.3 billion*, making it the highest moneymaker ever for the superhero genre and one of the biggest money-making movies of all time. And, for Steve, here was a movie that had it all: a creation story of a mythical African kingdom, strong male and female characters rooted in their primal power but still connected to their emotional core, and a techno-futuristic African society that had never been colonized and was still rooted in African tribal traditions.

"In *Black Panther*, we had a main character, T'Challa, who was a king who had lost his father. But rather than wallow in the tragedy, he was a connected adult: an aware, powerful human being rooted in intellect and body. It was something we need to see . . . just like women said about *Wonder Woman*," shared Barnes.

For those not familiar, the movie presents a compelling and powerful story. It depicts an African superhero in his home kingdom of Wakanda. Wakanda is a secret kingdom hidden from the rest of the world still keeping alive ancient traditions of connection to nature, tribe, and ancestors, but it also possesses cutting-edge technology that derives from a special metal, named vibranium, that allows Wakandan scientists, like T'Challa's sister Shuri, to create wondrous technological marvels, including T'Challa's secret Black Panther armor/suit.

The imagery and story of the film is intense, evocative, beautiful, and epic. At different points in the story, characters journey to the ancestral spirit world through the use of a sacred medicinal herb given to them by African tribal shamans. There they look upon the great African savannah (the same one we keep trying to groom our parks into) and meet their ancestors, who offer sage advice on their current modern predicaments. Different Wakandan tribal groups live in or out of their capital city, dressed in tribal garb carrying science-fiction level technology, but are also intimately connected with their herding and nomadic traditions. At one point, one of the characters even brings a herd of rhinos into battle. It's like they've found the secret to keeping their primal, original natures alive and still be in touch with ancestral traditions but are wildly successful in the modern world, too. This ideal appeals strongly to me, even if I'm not African-American, and may hold a key to how we can go forward carrying our primal natures in the 21st century.

In the film, male and female characters are both depicted as powerful primal beings in touch with their physicality, but also intellectually and emotionally balanced. King T'Challa is protected by numerous female bodyguards, takes advice from his matronly queen mother, has a secret agent romantic interest, and is equally teased and advised by his high-tech protégé sister. These powerful female characters serve as strong role models for any young women, including my daughters.

"With *Black Panther,* you had a movie about black people in and of themselves. *Black Panther* was different, and it acknowledged history. But it was not in relation to white people. In it, you had characters connected to their ancestors and were fully realized human beings. It resolved male and female, black and white. It helped answer the question, 'What is it to be a human being?' It was an event, not just a movie, and it satisfied a hunger gnawing at us for four centuries," Steven summarized.

We all have these internal things gnawing at us: our primal longings for tribe and village, for unimpeded time in pristine nature, for wild food gathered by hand, for dancing around the fire at night, and even for deep physical challenge. Movies on big screens have become a form of modern mythology echoing stories shared around the fire centuries ago. Archetypal images dance in our minds, evoking and provoking new thoughts, ideas, and ways of being. So much of these stories are about possibilities, whether it's the ancient story of the soot-covered boy who defeated the North Wind and became a hero for his people or the story of the kingdom of Wakanda peopled with heroes who successfully straddle the ancient primal wisdom of their ancestors and the unbelievable assets of their nearly magical technological gifts.

Stories like *Black Panther* have a lot to teach us about how we might successfully navigate and integrate our wild, primal selves with the complexity of our modern technological world. Perhaps it is possible to fully remember our ancient human history and integrate our primal, wild longings.

Chapter 8

Free-Range Children: Kids Being Rewilded

A Free Range Kid is a kid who gets treated as a smart, young, capable individual, not an invalid who needs constant attention and help.
—Lenore Skenazy, author of *Free Range Kids: How to Raise Safe, Self-Reliant Children (Without Going Nuts with Worry)*

My family didn't really camp. This is a surprise to a lot of people who know me, given my life's work being out in nature. But as a kid, I probably only slept in a tent outside once before I was a teenager. But I did enjoy nature in other ways.

My early childhood experiences were filled with epic outside adventures with buddies of mine playing at a nearby pond. We would catch frogs, fish, and turtles, and then let them go. We created secret maps of the tiny patch of woods near the pond, and we would sneak along the fence lines of the nearby golf course to watch rabbits, squirrels, and even an occasional owl. I didn't realize it at the time, but I was one of the last generations of truly Free Range kids allowed to wander and play in nature almost at will.

I might not have camped much, but outside time in nature was a core part of being a kid, and I was primed for a deeper connection.

By the time I went to the Ancient Lifeways Institute at age 13, I was psyched to be sleeping in reconstructed longhouses and other types of natural shelters. I felt so alive being in the open air almost 24 hours a day. But it was the annual overnight mini-expedition that excited me the most.

Often before heading out on our overnight, we were given only a short period of time to get ready, and with little or no warning. Instead of bringing tents and lots of equipment, we would cram our sleeping bags into our daypacks (with no sleeping pads) and hike from the main site at ALI to our overnight location: a rock overhang. This huge, granite slab that must have weighed thousands of pounds served as our shelter for the night. Jonah and Watie, our trusted instructors, guided us there each year and watched over us, and, while we didn't have as formal an oral tradition as we did most nights, we had some fun stories and silliness around the campfire.

And for some reason we always heard coyotes—every single time. At the time, I wondered if we were disturbing them because we were near their core territory. Often, they sounded incredibly close, and we suburban kids got pretty nervous. Eventually they would die down, and we were often treated to an amazing night of watching stars and stories of the constellations from our instructors.

We would wake up the next morning with plenty of energy, even if we didn't actually sleep that well (a phenomenon known to campers worldwide), and we would set off on a different route back to ALI. Over time, I began to notice that the route we chose to head back along always had a big patch of stinging nettle that we had to hike through. We were given little or even no warning, and for myself and others, the stinging sensations on our uncovered legs or arms were often an intense introduction on how to identify nettle. We learned to avoid it carefully, or else wear long pants and sleeves to be protected.

These kinds of experiences of being thrown into a scenario with little or no warning, preparation, and equipment were a core part of how we were taught at Ancient Lifeways, and it is this type of experience that sits strongly in my childhood memories.

Sometimes we were given lots of instruction on how to do something, sometimes very little. Our questions were sometimes answered, but often met with other questions or even a simple, "Why don't you try it and see if you can figure it out?"

I didn't realize it at the time, but there was something very deliberate and specific going on with how we were being taught and mentored. I learned years later that we deliberately hiked through nettles every year to create awareness, resilience, and adaptability. And the coyotes were part of the awareness training, as well, often lured into loud, vocal back-and-forth with a recording of coyotes played, unbeknownst to us, by one of the instructors not far from the rock slab where we set up camp.

❧

When I was 19, I made my first journey to the Pacific Northwest. I spent the summer on the idyllic Vashon Island teaching at a residential summer camp called Camp Sealth. It was my first exposure to the West Coast and really eye-opening. I fell in love with old growth trees, mountain landscapes, and feasting on wild berries. My job was to tend to young boys ages 6 to 8, and take them on fun, nature adventures. I'm not sure how good at it I really was at the time, but I was deeply touched by the joy and adventure of seeing kids spend time outside and to help gently facilitate the experience. It also awakened something deep in my soul.

During my time off from camp that summer, I went on my first backpacking trips to the Olympic Peninsula and the Cascade Mountains, where I swam in frigid mountain lakes, hiked on rocky sea-stacks under a full moon, and gorged myself on wild thimbleberries and oval-leafed blueberries. I was forever changed by these deep nature experiences with both kids and my friends.

I was discovering nature connection and my own primal journey. When I went back to college that fall, I continued to finish up my degrees in anthropology and Asian studies, but I also started taking as many ecology and environmental science classes as I could.

When I finished college a year or so later, my first job was at the oldest environmental education center in the United States: the Pocono Environmental Education Center or PEEC. PEEC was one of the first places in the country to bring kids in for residential, overnight school-year environmental education. By the time I was there, PEEC had been operating for 30 years. I joined a cadre of other just-out-of-college, highly idealistic, nature-loving folks as a team of educators for mostly fifth graders who would come from all over for a 3-day, 2-night nature immersion.

My fellow teachers and I led classes such as Forest Ecology, Pond Ecology, Beaver Studies, Night Hikes, and even took the kids on a low-ropes challenge course. Kids of all backgrounds came, and we had kids from the inner cities of both Philadelphia and New York City who had never been out of the city before. Our job was to inspire and teach them about nature, and to keep them safe. And it worked, for the most part.

During my time at PEEC, I became good friends with a man named Dan Rain. Dan was a recent college graduate like myself who was super passionate about environmental issues, but who was also really into this guy named Tom Brown Jr. (whom I had only minimally heard about before Dan). Dan always took me out to look at animal tracks—something I hadn't really paid that much attention to before. But, soon, I was bitten by the tracking bug, and Dan and I would wake up early to come to track beavers, otters, and mink in the snow around a small pond before breakfast and an 8-hour day of teaching kids from the city. At night, we would sip on beers at our cabin, before we passed out from exhaustion and did the whole thing over again the next day.

Over time, Dan and I noticed some curious things about what we were teaching. I had gotten Dan more excited about survival skills just like he had gotten me excited about tracking. We also both really enjoyed taking kids on wildlife-stalking adventures or blindfolding them and doing sensory awareness games. In fact, the less structured we were with our classes, and the more we incorporated tracking, survival skills, edible plants, blindfold games, and the like, the more the kids seemed to stay engaged and love what they were doing. They also seemed to learn more during these unstructured moments.

Dan and I speculated about what it would be like to have 3 days with kids where all we did was build survival shelters, go tracking, stalk the pond looking for wildlife, and make meals out of wild edibles. In many ways, we were designing primal adventures for our students that mimicked our own longings and connections with our hunter-gatherer nature. We incorporated these ideas as much as we could, but eventually our time at PEEC came to an end; it was time for me to head back west to Seattle. But it was at the suggestion of longtime PEEC staff that I checked out a place called Wilderness Awareness School.

During the next summer, I participated in a day camp taught in the Wilderness Awareness School style. I was a volunteer assistant, watching and adding in where I could. By the end of the day, I was hooked. Here was a program that took groups of kids out all day and taught survival skills, awareness, tracking, and medicinal and edible plants, and was doing it in a seamless, effortless fun-filled way that was nourishing for the kids and the instructors: primal, wild, and free-range for everybody. Each day felt like an adventure slowly building on the powerful fun, mythology, and ideas of the day before. We used bird language and stalking skills; made fire, cordage, and shelters; and wove storytelling, silliness, and adventures through it all. It didn't really feel or seem like teaching, more like we were all just having fun together.

Simultaneously at the same park where the day camp was held, Jon Young was teaching a week-long class for adults, called the Art of Mentoring. In this class, he laid out his and WAS's teaching philosophy and approach based on his upbringing with Tom Brown and with teachings from other people and places. The class was an immersion for homeschool parents, mentors, educators, and people wanting their kids to remain free range. I didn't realize that this was happening, nor did I realize that Jon had just started teaching this kind of class, having taught the first one of its kind back at PEEC about a month before I got there.

These two related programs—Jon's Art of Mentoring approach and WAS's application of it in youth programs—went global and created a powerful grassroots movement that challenged traditional notions of environmental education and education in general. This movement has combined with other styles of parenting and education, including Unschooling and the Free Range kids movement, to grow exponentially. Now it has entered the national discourse as people seek to free their kids from as many as 70-plus hours a week spent in front of screens.

What happens when children are reconnected with nature? How relevant are survival skills for kids in the 21st century? And what happens when we start to rewild children by the tens of thousands? Can we have primal kids and families?

While WAS and Jon Young are some of the key players in the rewilding/free-range child movement, there are plenty of other voices and players in what is truly a rising global mission. I reached out to different people and voices and players in this field to gain their insights into what is going on and why.

Tony Deis started one of the most creative and successful youth programs that focuses on rewilding kids around the world. The fast-speaking, loquacious, and prolific Tony Deis (not unlike his *Avengers* namesake, Tony Stark, aka Iron Man—a comparison that Tony doesn't shy away from) started Trackers NW in 2004, which eventually turned into Trackers Earth, in Portland, Oregon. Tony spent his teenage years trying to find an educational system that would match his talents and skills after the public school system failed him. He spent some time at WAS and the Tracker

School, and eventually took the skills of tracking, survival, and nature connection, and combined it with his own flavor of family- and community-based programming to create what might be the most successful survival skills programs for kids in the world. His summer camps and kids programs combine survival skills, nature connection, and elements of pop culture to create some of the most creative camps around, including a Wizards, Giants, and Elves camp; a Pirate Camp; and a Secret Agent summer camp.

If this sounds a little over the top, all we need to do is take a look at the numbers. In 2006, two years after starting Trackers NW only had forty students enrolled in their summer programs, but by 2018, combining their numbers from their programs in the Bay Area and Portland (their two locations), they reached over 18,000 kids *just in the summer*. And, if you include their year-round programming and adult participants, then they reach over 23,000 students per year. This is unprecedented growth in just over a decade.

Tony's programs create purpose for people beyond our tendency toward self-centeredness. This includes creating space and time for family and village, exploring diversity in the human and natural world, emphasis on our relationships with the more-than-human world (such as plants, animals, trees, rivers and forest), and awareness beyond our lifetime acknowledging our past and looking forward to future generations coming after us. At Trackers Earth, instructors dress up like pirates or wizards and enact complex mythological scenarios, all while teaching people about survival skills, plant medicines, and other ways to connect to nature.

So why the rapid growth? Why is this kind of work so important right now?

"On the grandest scale," Tony explained, "we are working to correct the erroneous habits and assumptions, the memes, that 10,000 years of toxic human expansion has put upon this planet and all other species we share it with. Though we do recognize that such dramatic change may not be likely—at least in our lifetime—we work to provide connections that assail one of the greatest epidemics of our time: isolation and loneliness."

This theme popped up in numerous interviews with people who work with kids and adults. The goal is to provide a deep, restorative, regenerative connection to nature and our ancient longings while also providing that same kind of connection to people in the form of community. Primal longings include a desire for other humans in a connected way and even include a desire for multigenerational play and interaction.

"This propensity towards isolation or communal disparity is perpetuated by poor habits and lack of experience," Tony shared. "Nature connection helps us reacquire those skills that make us human. We are a species that evolved to possess a high degree of inter-subjectivity, which facilitates communal-based survival strategies. Returning to those roots—or at least practicing them—provides hands-on routines that form healthier habits and the experience to forge more resilient communal and familial bonds."

But it's not just about community and connection; there's also a healthy dose of fun and adventure that's underneath it all.

"Finally, beyond the value to the greater community, individuals can form better habits of restoring old, and creating new, social connections for better personal health and functional resiliency. Plus, wild foods are fun to find and eat. And they are free. Campfires are cool too," Tony summarized.

Tony created this out of what was missing from his own education growing up. He started a business that would provide kids with adventure, excitement, learning, and growth. Trackers Earth has now become a major player in the Portland area, transforming the life and experience of thousands of children every year. And it's not just making a difference for kids; Trackers now provides jobs for fifty full-time educators with year-round wages, benefits, and decent pay.

Why are parents sending their kids to these programs in droves? Do parents think their kids need these skills, or is it the novel ideas behind the camps that bring people in?

"I believe that the novelty is not necessarily the draw," Tony said. "People innately want their kids to be more resilient and autonomous. They also recognize adventure . . . [these are also] innate and very human skills. Parents feel it's necessary for their kids to have these skills . . . and it helps create a sense of place and connection to the wilder world."

But in today's world, where our kids are exposed to screens and digital technology earlier and earlier, how do we make this technology and our underlying primal longings and desires work in concert together?

"[Apps and social media] are utilizing evolutionary adaptations in our brain. Apps use a reward system and social system that mimic real connections we long for. It's like the empty calories of sugar, salt, and fat that are actually devoid of nutritional value. . . . People sense that emptiness, that isolation. This is not true nutrition for the body or for the soul. It's not nutrition for the spirit or for our mental health."

When we get back to our primal nature and pursue survival skills, nature connection, and a sense of adventure, we satisfy those longings that apps and social media exploit. Wilderness skills, holistic food, and community become interconnected, and it's that connectedness that we crave.

"Apps and social media create a lack of satiation and represent 'empty calories,'" Tony further explained. "They are not a true multi-sensory experience. But, when you combine survival skills [with] community, the combination is much more enjoyable and has a pragmatic value in our daily lives. Most people are simply looking for connection and adventure that they can co-create with a team of people and that they can create for themselves."

Trackers Earth's growth phenomenon is not an isolated incident. Survival programs across the country have seen exponential growth. Wilderness Awareness School's youth programs and summer camps went through a growth curve similar to Trackers during the late 90s and early 2000s. Programs exploded all over the Puget Sound area near Seattle. These multi-age summer camp experiences soon extended into the school year, with weekly programs for teens and homeschool kids. Kids of all ages were deeply connecting to nature, learning survival skills, and having lots of fun and adventures along the way.

But, while the West Coast, with its lush forests, mountains, and rushing rivers, and environmentally focused populace and parents, might be very fertile grounds for kids to ignite their primal instincts in a summer camp setting, what about other areas of the country? What about, say, Texas?

This free-range phenomenon, as it turns out, doesn't stop at state borders. The desire to get outdoors is strengthening everywhere, and schools like Earth Native, in Austin, Texas, are quickly scaling up to supply the demand. Dave Scott, the founder and director of Earth Native, can trace his deep love for nature and the outdoors back to his earliest free-range childhood memories catching crayfish and minnows in the little creek behind the house he grew up in; hunting and fishing with his father and grandfather in Corpus Christi, Texas; riding horses with his brother in the Colorado Rockies; and building forts and engaging in imaginary play with his friends. After a childhood filled with outdoor exploration and adventure, Dave joined a search and rescue team in southern Colorado, where his passion for self-reliance and wilderness survival was further ignited through his experience helping others in wilderness emergencies.

After a 6-year stint in the military, Dave began pursuing his passion for the outdoors full-time, studying wilderness survival, wildlife tracking, youth and adult mentoring, naturalist studies, and sustainable living skills at wilderness schools across the country.

Dave's free-range childhood, one in which he and his brother were free to roam and play in the quarter-mile of woods behind their Austin home (as long as they could hear their mom when she called) had lasting impacts on his life and his life's work.

Like Dave, I was lucky enough to spend a childhood immersed in nature. Even though I grew up in the environmentally challenged landscape of Illinois (dominated by corn and soybeans), I played barefoot and wild in the man-made pond and park-like settings of a mild midwestern suburban setting. It was the norm back then to kick children out of the household to go play in a little patch of nature, such as a small forest, creek, or nearby pond. I grew up fishing. My childhood consisted of being barefoot, swimming and wading in the creeks and pond, and catching frogs, fish, crayfish, and turtles. This was the norm for me and most of my contemporaries—before television had more than three to five channels and before video games became sophisticated, three-dimensional multiplayer hours-sucking adventures.

This kind of free-range existence for kids nearly died out. As documented by Richard Louv in his work, *Last Child in the Woods*, during the 80s and 90s parents stopped letting their kids play outside so much, and on-screen entertainment, video games, and, later, the Internet began dominating kids' free time outside of school.

Programs such as Wilderness Awareness School, Trackers Earth, and Earth Native have basically grown to fill in this void. If Richard Louv identified Nature Deficit Disorder, then programs like these are the remedy. And how are they working?

Dave's Earth Native programs are modeled heavily after his own childhood experiences, mixed together with the survival skills and teaching philosophy he learned at WAS and through teachers like Jon Young.

These programs are designed to help kids get outside, get off their devices, and reconnect with nature, themselves, and their communities. Recent studies have shown that some children are now spending upwards of *70 hours per week in front of screens.* While Earth Native doesn't have quite the same breadth of reach as Trackers Earth, Dave does like to point to other ways to measure their success. Last year, Earth Native had *70,000 hours of field time of children connecting in nature*, a powerful counter-measure indeed.

But can you really get kids to leave behind all of the Minecraft and Fortnite talk? Can you really get them to disconnect from social media and reconnect to nature?

"I've definitely seen that kids are more digitally and media-focused over the last 8 years," Dave said. "I used to assume that you are either a kid that plays video games or you go out in nature. But that's not really the case. Every kid is both. You can talk about Minecraft and then spend time in nature getting connected."

However, Dave is quick to mention how instinctual and powerful this form of education, mentoring, and play is for kids.

"One could make an argument, as I often do, that in order for our family lines to have continued to this point, every one of us is the descendant of the best, most capable hunters, trackers, and survival skills practitioners," said Dave.

Literally, we are descended from the people who were successful with these most ancient and primal skills. And our kids naturally want to learn these things, too. It is ingrained in their DNA.

"Children are not dissimilar to other young creatures on the Earth. Each animal spends its childhood intent on learning and understanding the world in which it lives and the resources that it takes to survive. It is my belief that children have a natural interest in outdoor survival skills because they have an instinctual drive to learn these vital ancestral skills," pointed out Dave.

"Almost all children are inspired by the same things in the outdoors, the same things that I was also inspired about as a child—things like fire building and tending; building stick forts; gathering and eating wild edible plants; catching fish, frogs, snakes, and other things; throwing rocks and sticks; and many others. Almost all of these children's passions can pretty easily be connected back to actual vital skills that our forbearers were using not that many generations ago for their survival."

What happens when kids are allowed to play and develop this way?

It's not an easy question to answer. But there are lots of things Dave, Tony, and I have seen over the years. Kids become more poised, more at ease. They are resilient and have an incredible ability to learn in different contexts and ways. They tend to develop deep respect for each other, for life, and for the world around them. And, just like adults who experience deep nature connection, they tend to become happier, healthier, and smarter. A lot of parents seem to know this and seek out these kinds of programs for their kids.

"Honestly, I think that, just as there is an instinctual drive within children to be outside, there is an instinctual drive for parents to take their children outdoors. As a parent, I have found the feedback I get from my children in the form of growth and development to be more than enough motivation to encourage outdoor play," summarized Dave.

As a parent, educator, and mentor, I've seen these things in my own kids as well as others. I've also seen some pretty radical things that really upend some of our basic notions about education, development, and special needs kids. Anecdotally, over the years one of the most amazing things that I and many of my peers have seen is that many kids who have been labeled with ADD, ADHD, or even some form of autism-spectrum disorder thrive in a deep nature connection program like the ones described above. *Sometimes kids who have these labels actually thrive and excel at skills like tracking, bird language, and stalking.* I've also seen them come into one of these programs unable to function in a classroom setting due to a diagnosis of ADD or ADHD and then leave the program after a year or two and be able to go back into a classroom setting and be successful.

While this may be hard to believe, these kinds of results are being found in other situations and contexts, as well. Temple Grandin, a highly successful PhD biologist who is a self-described autist (singular for autistic), is able to work with her autistic tendencies primarily through her connection with animals, and her work shows that it is highly likely that autistic kids and adults have a much higher aptitude for communicating and connecting with animals than the rest of us. In fact, autism as we understand it may be less of a diagnosis or problem than we've been led to believe and more of a gift of an extremely tuned in, aware, and sensitive person.

This idea is further explored in Rupert Isaacson's book and film, *The Horse Boy*. In both the book and the film, Isaacson documents in clear detail his son's remarkable transformation and his own family's battle with their son's autism diagnosis and behavior. Over time, Isaacson finds that his son responds best to time in nature and time on horseback or with horses. Horses that are normally hostile, aggressive, or difficult to deal with become docile around Rupert's son, Rowan. Isaacson is deeply connected to Bushmen communities in his native South Africa. After some tentative success in healing from the Bushmen and other shamanic healers, Rowan, Rupert, and Rowan's mom, Kristin, set out on an epic journey to Mongolia to find healing through one of the last remaining horse cultures and through their native reindeer and horse shamans. The family has been successful in their quest to create massive changes for Rowan through time in nature, immersion in a horse culture, and shamanic healing. Dave Scott's brother, Michael, was the filmmaker that helped them document their journey.

Deep nature connection and survival skills training are good for our kids, who have their own primal, hunter-gatherer instincts that are not too far below the surface. You can run very successful programs using this as the basis for your model. And very compelling anecdotal evidence suggests some of these things might be incredibly effective in working with kids or adults who have autism, ADD, ADHD, or other related "disorders."

Rewilding Schools Everywhere

There are now hundreds, perhaps thousands, of schools and programs around the world using deep nature connection routines and
survival skills to help rewild children and allow them to be more
free-range, alive, and natural. I am unaware of an exhaustive list of
all the programs using these methods, and it's beyond the scope
of this book to try to compile one. Most of the organizations and
people in this book do also work with youth, and besides the really
big players, like Wilderness Awareness School, Trackers Earth, and
Earth Native, there are many other models and styles of integrating
these principles. There is a growing movement of Forest Kindergar-
tens or Forest Preschools around the country and around the world.
TinyTrees is an organization in the Seattle area that seeks to provide
outdoor preschool education for free for any family that wants it.
Feather and Frond Forest School in Bellingham, Washington, is
another example of an outdoor preschool with mixed-age programming available for older kids, as well. These forest preschools are
just the precursor to the soon-to-be growing forest schools, where
kids learn all of their core subjects but spend most of their time in
an outdoor setting. For example, Trackers Earth has started a full
5-day-a-week forest school for elementary, middle, and high school
kids. They just recently developed a teacher training program to
train forest school teachers to create the staff they need and for
other similar programs that will hopefully develop soon.

But what happens when people grow up being deeply mentored in a natural wild primal way? How are they able to function
in the world? What kind of success, failures, and challenges do
they face out in the rest of the world once they leave the "nest" of
deep nature connection programs and the survival skills world?

While there is no one particular answer to this question and
results vary, there are a lot of amazing stories of students who
have spent time in long-term immersion programs like those
described in this book who've gone on to wonderful, wild, careers
creating positive impacts for themselves and their communities. In

particular, the Community School—a high school–age program based at WAS for teenagers focusing on deep nature connection, community, and survival skills—has served for over 20 years as a "lab school" for what is possible when people are immersed in these programs for some time.

A few things stand out time and again about the Community School students and grads. One is the incredible way these teenagers treat each other. While, like teenagers everywhere, there is typical experimentation with drugs, alcohol, and sex, there is very little of the bickering, bullying, putting down, or intense social drama that is present in so many teenagers around the country. Students tend to treat each other and the world around them with respect, while deeply pursuing what they are passionate about.

In fact, the Community School students and the qualities that they displayed were key in drawing Gilbert Walking Bull, the Lakota elder mentioned earlier, to living and working at WAS for over a decade. Gilbert saw natural sacred qualities emerging in these kids. He identified things like seeing them being truly helpful to one another and the world, or the capacity for deep self-sufficiency, or even retaining their natural deep wonder and curiosity at the world without becoming jaded as they transitioned into adults.

The students' own natural gifts and capacities rose to the surface. One student found his passion in woodworking and went on to build world-class award-winning violins and cellos. Another went on to set up his own blacksmithing business. Others have gone to Yale or Harvard. One young woman I know went on to get a PhD in international relations focusing on genocide prevention, building on what she learned about conflict resolution and communication while at WAS. Other students have gone on to join the circus or even start their own businesses.

One of the grads from those early days is Doniga Markegard. Doniga went to Community School in the late 90s, and she documents her journey as a student along with her own journey of self-discovery in her book, *Dawn Again*. Since the Community School, Doniga has gone on to study wildlife biology, permaculture, and regenerative agriculture and ranching, and she currently runs a huge, successful ranching operation with her husband in Northern California. Doniga integrates all that she learned at WAS and Community School to successfully help manage the ranch, raise her three kids, and author books.

Doniga helps build her kids to be resilient, strong, flexible, and dynamic by raising them free-range on the ranch. Tracking, moving cattle, nature connection, mapping, bird language, and survival skills all work together to create a healthy, robust microbiome for the kids, their family, and the planet. Doniga sees that this kind of work is vital for her family and the world.

"I feel it is my duty to set my kids up with the strongest immune system possible, and this does not come from a sterile environment," she said. "We have kids groups out to the ranch, and some have never touched a chicken. . . . Lifestyle plays a big part. The work our family does is tangible. We use our hands to create something—food that feeds people and communities. We are surrounded by nature, and our agriculture practices enhance nature. Kids need to see more adults working with their bodies and the land to create. Our kids are connecting with their senses. When we check on the cattle, we stop to look at tracks. We play in the mud, and we sleep out under the stars."

Doniga's work plays a big role in the mental health of her kids and other kids, as well. Their mental health has been positively impacted by their regular nature connections. As a result, the kids are innately able to tap into their intuition, their passions, and even face down stress and fear in a positive, healthy way.

I asked Doniga about her own parenting style. How do she and her husband raise their children on a cattle ranch?

"We have very free-ranging children. We have worked hard to impart values of love for each other and the earth. . . . From there they are able to explore, play, learn, and follow their curiosities.

Since we live in an area with a lot of wide open space, their backyard is limitless. They have a large area in the forest where they have built forts. We want our kids to be able to work hard and play hard."

Doniga's writing and her work at the ranch have now enabled her to travel around the world to study regenerative farm and food practices. The holistic ranching model the ranch has adopted is garnering international attention, as well, as people see the interplay of family, ranch, farm, and food in a way that is regenerating everyone and the land itself. Doniga grew up as part of the first generation of kids being deliberately rewilded, and now uses that same philosophy to raise her own children, run a business, and positively impact the planet.

Okay, so rewilding our kids, letting them be free-range, and giving them ample time in nature seems to be good for them, and it can create healthy, functioning successful adults. But how does this relate to actual hunter-gatherers? What are hunter-gatherer childhoods really like?

I knew the perfect person to ask about this very topic. Sheina Lew-Levy is a former student of WAS, and she is now pursuing her PhD in psychology from the University of Cambridge. Her thesis is focused on hunter-gatherer childhoods.

Sheina's story, just like a lot of people in this book, is quite remarkable, but *unlike* a lot of the other people I talked to she didn't have a childhood immersed in nature—quite the opposite, actually. Around preschool age, Sheina was misdiagnosed as being developmentally delayed. She had been placed in a class of students a grade ahead of where she should have been placed, and, being the child of two first-generation immigrants, she didn't speak English well at that early age. Her parents were both academics (her dad an anthropologist and her mom a psychiatrist), and they were understandably quite concerned. As Sheina describes it, they overcompensated by filling her grade school years with tutors, extra classes, and lots of extra studies.

"I was kind of schooled and homeschooled at the same time," Sheina jokingly shared.

Sheina distinctly remembers longing to play outside with her sister and friends but instead suffered through extra French lessons, piano, ballet, and other extra academic activities. In the midst of all this learning, Sheina was diagnosed with a learning disability that she describes as kind of the reverse of dyslexia. She can read, write, and comprehend fine, but occasionally she can't remember specific words or switches words for objects. She also specifically describes a high level of personal clumsiness that may or may not be related (and which could be a result of a lack of unstructured outdoor play).

In the midst of this highly structured and academic environment, Sheina's outlet was to explore hands-on craft activities, such as knitting and fiber arts. As she got older, she got curious about early human tool use and primitive skills. Eventually, she took some primitive skills classes and met Steve Leckman (who would later go on to form Coyote Programmes and work with Native and non-Native groups in Quebec). After realizing her love for survival skills, Sheina joined the Anake program and flourished and excelled at skills like bow-drill, tracking, and related arts. There are insights and aspects of the experience that still linger with her today. In particular, Sheina sees the program as providing solid hands-on science learning.

"I think friction fire is the root of technology. When you take friction fire to its ignition point, then it's physics and science you can see with your eyes. You can learn science in a classroom but you don't learn them in your body. Primitive skills might be the best way to make a bunch of scientists."

While Sheina excelled at WAS both in the Anake program and as an apprentice instructor, it's what she's done since she's left that's really outstanding and helps us understand the connection between the rewilding/free-range kid movement and actual contemporary hunter-gatherer children. When Sheina left WAS, she went back to finish her undergraduate degree, and she quickly seized opportunities to go and study with hunter-gatherer groups in different settings, including a 3-month field school in east Africa and a self-designed study looking at tracking culture among the native Cree people of northern Canada.

When in the classroom during her studies, Sheina had an insight about learning and how we learn. She suffered extreme boredom in a Swahili class that was heavily focused on repetition, memorization, and endless recitation. During the class, Sheina found herself reading blogs written by free-range moms discussing hunter-gatherer childhoods and how kids actually learn in those settings. It resonated with her, including her time at WAS, and she started to explore other ways of learning that reflected the nonhierarchical, nondidactic educational model she had experienced in the world of survival skills, and which was the *main* style of learning in hunter-gatherer groups.

During her time with the Cree, Sheina was able to talk to a female chieftain who was heavily involved with the reconstruction of their education and schooling. Her husband was part of the school board, as the Cree reindigenized and decolonized the previous boarding school model that they had suffered under for years. However, even though both parents were so involved with the formal education system, they regularly pulled their kids out of school to spend time on the land. Their son, in particular, just didn't excel in the formal school setting. One Cree elder responded to this by saying, "There's one in every family," meaning that it was understood that there was one high-level hunter and fisherman in each family that would need to be out in nature, unstructured, to grow and reach their full potential.

"With the Cree, they took their son out because he excelled as a hunter and fisher," Sheina explained. "Hunter-gatherers have a very different idea of multiple intelligences. And most hunter-gatherers see *children as autonomously gaining intelligence.* If you just let them be, they will get smarter. It doesn't have to be a formalized, structured process. There is a community and ecology of learning. It's like an invisible school. Things are happening around kids, and kids are paying attention."

Later, Sheina took this passion and inquiry to Cambridge, where she performed field research in the Congo, repeatedly studying hunter-gatherer childhoods as part of her thesis.

Plants were some of Sheina's passions when she was at WAS, and she got pretty good at learning almost all of the plants on the 20-plus-acre campus and their purposes. She thought she'd have no problem with plant identification in the Congo. Needless to say, Sheina was pretty surprised when she had to rely on 5-year-olds to teach her plants. In fact, one little girl was able to tell her the difference between two leaves that Sheina couldn't tell apart. One was edible and one wasn't, and, even with her previous training Sheina couldn't see the difference.

"I once heard Jon Young describe going through Anake as Bushmen kindergarten. I was kind of skeptical of that at first, but after my time in the Congo I understand what he was getting at," quipped Sheina.

By the age of 12, almost all of the kids in the Congo village were able to hunt and gather and help provide for the family. But how did the kids learn all of this by age 12?

Well, it wasn't by sitting in a classroom and being lectured to all day. The main way the children learn is through play.

Most of the play the children are engaged in is imitation of adult activity. They pretend to cook, play house, make spears, and chase other kids. In fact, I've found that if you leave kids alone in nature with minimal supervision they very quickly start spontaneously playing in ways that develop survival skills and hunter-gatherer core activities. Kids build forts (making shelter), pretend to make fire, chase each other, make spears or bows and arrows, gather plants, make potions (practicing pretend herbal medicine), and so forth. In the Congo, the kids did similar things, only they had grown up hunter-gatherers to watch, imitate, and learn from continually.

Sheina also observed unique social aspects of play, such as pretending to share an animal that one has hunted by breaking up a branch into different pieces for different people. Sharing is a core part of the egalitarian nature of hunter-gatherer groups who have to rely on each other. No one is successful hunting and gathering as an individual all the time. Sharing and reciprocity is also a vital survival skill (this is an important point we will look at later). The play among the hunter-gatherer Congo children also involved lots of intense vigorous physical activities, such as running, jumping, climbing, and imitating animals—the ultimate original natural movement and exercise. Sheina described regularly seeing 12-year-olds with natural eight-pack abs from their play.

Finally, play is a form of practicing innovation. Humans need culture, flexibility, and innovation to succeed in life, no matter what the setting, and often this experimentation begins in childhood as kids try out things differently from what they see the adults doing. The kids in the Congo village tried out experiments and told the adults what worked and what didn't. They also spent time as the eyes and ears of the village, noticing tracks, food plants, and rare food sources, such as honey, while they wandered and roamed near the adults and just outside the village.

One of the biggest differences Sheina noticed among the kids in the Congo was a lack of competitive play and games. When you have a mixed-age group of kids from 3 to 16, it's difficult and not very productive for kids to play against each other. Instead, there were lots of cooperative activities, games, and play. This carries into adulthood, where there is little or no competition, as everybody needs to rely on each other. For Sheina, this is an important observational point.

"Structuring a non-competitive, multi-age group for education could have huge positive benefits for individuals and society."

How different might things be if we all were working together to share resources and celebrating everybody's successes?

I asked Sheina to reflect on her own learning journey with WAS, with overcoming a learning disability, and on facing the rigors of the intense academic environment of graduate-level studies at Cambridge. She was able to see them all as interconnected.

"At WAS, I felt like I was finally in a place where I wasn't being assessed. I was able to play with things without feeling like there needed to be an outcome. I was nervous about different things, but I found experiences of resiliency at WAS that were really, truly self-motivated . . . things I did for myself. This sense of resiliency and self-motivation has followed me into academia. And failure, learning to fail. It's okay to fuck up from time to time!" said Sheina.

"WAS filled me with so many questions that I was desperate to answer. My advisors are always trying to convince me to do less. But I'm so filled with passion and excitement. There is a sense of fullness and leading from a place of passion. I found that I made these choices, and I like them. I may have failed at different times, but I still found it interesting, cool, and fun."

Parents may wonder what all this means for their child and their education. How do you rewild children and raise them to be successful in our current system? And do kids actually learn anything when they're running wild and free, engaging in their natural primal instincts, being guided by mentors along the way?

While there isn't a specific answer, I'll share two stories from my own life that can shed some light on the topic. The first story involves a young woman named Avi Stein. When Avi was a teen, she fell in love with WAS and its approach, especially after a memorable summer tracking reintroduced wild wolves in the rugged wilderness of Idaho. With her parents' blessing, Avi joined the WAS Community School program and took a break from regular high school (though she did keep up with some outside studies). Later, after a few years of being fully immersed, Avi returned to high school, finishing and graduating with her peers. Around the time she graduated, Avi found herself at an environmental conference in Oregon. Avi had become passionate about environmental issues and found that it was a bridge to keep her connected to the wild side of herself as she navigated mainstream high school.

At the conference, Avi ended up in a class someone was teaching on edible and medicinal plants. Less than 20 minutes into the class, Avi and the teacher became aware of a glaring truth: Avi knew way more about plants than the teacher did. It's pretty remarkable that a teenager had more ethnobotanical knowledge than the professional educator. But here's the really amazing thing: Avi wasn't very interested in plants while she was at WAS, and she couldn't, for the life of her, explain how it was that she knew so much about plants. She had been passionate about tracking and wolves, and occasionally about fire-making and some other survival skills, but somewhere along the way, just by participating, she had learned graduate school–level knowledge of native plants and their uses. So, while kids may not realize just how much knowledge they're retaining, it is clear that rewilding and free-range approaches do educate.

The other story I want to share involves my daughter, Katie. Katie grew up at WAS, and even before she formally entered the programs there, my students and some of the WAS apprentices played with her and became her adopted aunties and uncles. Katie entered the preschool program at WAS, and she loved listening to birds, building giant nests on the ground, searching for fairies in the forest, and going on adventures to places with names like Buttslide Hill. When it came time for Katie to enter kindergarten, her mom and I chose to enroll her in public school. This surprised a lot of people who assumed we would just homeschool her, but that wasn't realistic, given that I was working full-time at WAS and her mom was a doctor.

Over time, Katie continued to grow and blossom, both at WAS, which she continued 1 day a week, and at public elementary school. In second grade, she placed into the Program for the Academically Talented (or PAT), an accelerated magnet program for elementary school kids in the valley where I live. Up until that point, Katie's teachers had been fine with her taking 1 day a week to be at WAS, as she was easily able to keep up with whatever assignments that were given to her. However, now that she was in the PAT program, there was resistance. I insisted that her teachers allow her to continue at WAS and at least give it a try.

Guess what? She continued to thrive. The first year, she was at or near the top of her class in the PAT program in math, science, reading, and pretty much everything else (while also doing gymnastics).

But the next year, Katie had a teacher who would just not budge—she refused to accept that it was okay for Katie to be at WAS 1 day a week. She thought Katie's performance would suffer. So what did I do? I pulled her out of class 1 day a week anyway, facing persecution and harassing calls from the principal and the school office about Katie's attendance.

But Katie proved them all wrong. Her grades actually got better. By the end of her fourth grade year, Katie was reading at a high school level and doing sixth and seventh grade math, all the while "wasting her time 1 day a week doing that nature school stuff." I wonder what would have happened if the whole school spent 1 day a week with the kids immersed in nature being rewilded and free-range.

Some countries, like Finland, Norway, and Sweden, have implemented radical educational policies over the last 10 to 15 years. In the face of falling test scores in math and science, they boosted rather than reduced recess time, and they have reintroduced mandatory outside time at school. This is radically different than the US approach, where we continue to cut time for recess and have little or no formal regular nature education, and, yet, our test scores continue to fall or plateau.

Linda McGurk, a Swedish-American mother, documents her own battles with these two different cultural views in her book, *There's No Such Thing as Bad Weather: A Scandinavian Mom's Secrets for Raising Healthy, Resilient, and Confident Kids*. McGurk shared struggles she has rectifying these two radically different approaches, such as the time she was nearly arrested for letting her kids play in a stream. Ultimately, she found a way to make it work by taking her daughters to Sweden for 6 months and figuring out a way to raise her own resilient, healthy kids in the face of adversity.

The Scandinavian approach has some serious merit: Finland, Norway, and Sweden consistently have some of the highest test scores for their kids' academic performance in the world (especially since implementing more nature time), and their adults also experience some of the highest degrees of happiness and life and work satisfaction.

Maybe we all need to be rewilded and a little more free-range.

CHAPTER 9

Our Longing for a Village

WHILE THE CONTENTS OF THIS BOOK MAY APPEAR SUPER SERI-
ous, one of the things I've learned over the years is that it is way
too easy to take things too seriously. A lot of people, including
many of the students I've worked with over the years, think that I
live in some off-grid self-sufficient cabin, and that I hunt, gather,
and grow all my own food. While those ideas are very appealing
to me, and, to some degree, that is the trajectory I want for my life,
it's also not the reality I experience. My family and I live in a mod-
est house in a small town in the Seattle suburbs. Yes, we can walk
to a river nearby with active salmon runs and resident bald eagles.
Yes, we do harvest rainwater, grow lots of berries in our yard, and
forage for food and medicine. But we also have to deal with the
sounds of leaf-blowers, and my neighbors get annoyed at me if I
don't mow my lawn often enough (which probably happens all the
time, since I mow it very, very infrequently).

Often, when I've hung out with friends from this field of
work, we do gather around a fire or go hiking or have a community potluck with some people bringing wild foods. But we also
go and see the latest superhero movies or talk about politics. Most
everybody I know in the field is also on social media or has a
webpage. Being web-savvy and having a social media presence is a
modern survival skill, for sure. In fact, one of the things some of us

have done outside of work over the years is get together and watch Seahawks football. In fact, a few years ago when the Seahawks won the Super Bowl, most of the WAS staff was there to watch the game at Warren Moon's house on his big-screen television.

A student once asked me a great question: "Nate, what do you see as something in our modern lives that has made things better for people and for the world?"

The student's question was not just a thoughtful and meaningful one, but it had a message for me, as well. Ultimately, underneath the obvious part of the question were deeper questions:

"Nate, do you see anything about our modern world that's actually better? Do you really think that we were all better off as hunter-gatherers? Should we just abandon everything from modernity and try to return to our ancient past?"

The student had a point. And I know that sometimes when I've talked about these things to different audiences it can seem like I'm advocating for abandoning our modern world and that I'm idealizing the past or hunter-gatherer lives. I can see how people would come to this conclusion from the kinds of things I talk about and the things I've done and taught for decades. But that's not exactly the message I'm trying to send.

On so many levels, both for people and the planet, it's totally impractical for us to suddenly give up our modern way of life and try to revert to hunter-gatherers. For one thing, most people would be horribly unsuccessful, and, for another, there's nowhere near enough intact food resources to feed all of us in a hunter-gatherer manner (wild animals and wild ecosystems are taxed enough already right now). Even a slow, gradual return to that life and lifestyle would be a multigenerational project with no true guarantee of success.

But it is possible for us to start living our lives more deliberately and more consciously aware of these deep primal impulses and instincts. In fact, if we did, it might be significantly better for people and the planet.

There's a vision of the future available to us where we integrate and become aware of our hunter-gatherer primal nature. In this future, we could design and create a regenerative society with the best of both worlds. In this world, ecosystems would be restored through collective, healthy, smart food practices. People could gather around fires at night and celebrate their adventures out on a wild landscape, but could also have access to computers, hi-tech medicine, and other aspects and developments of the modern world. We could find a way to walk continuously in Ingwe's two worlds or create a world based on the idea of Wakanda: integrated hunter-gatherer knowledge and instincts along with cutting-edge technology that rejuvenates and regenerates the land and ecosystems.

Not that long ago I was talking with a group of random strangers about the ideas presented in this book. It was around the winter holidays and everyone was in a chatty and gregarious mood. The group was from different backgrounds, with most of them hi-tech workers employed with Amazon or Microsoft. The ideas I was presenting resonated with all of them, and they realized that they had the very longings I was describing. Then, a gentleman hanging out on the periphery of our conversation chimed in.

"I agree with what you're saying, Nate," he said. "And, to be honest, I've worked for the advertising industry for a few decades. What you're describing is actually common knowledge behind closed doors. These primal impulses are what people use to sell things—it's kind of a way of hacking into people's subconscious brains."

So, why can't we hack into our subconscious primal needs and instincts in a conscious way to create a healthier, satisfying life, society, and planet?

I believe it is totally possible to understand our deep primal longings and integrate them into our lives. If we did so, we would all be happier and healthier, and would make better decisions on how to live on the planet and how to live with one another.

Perhaps for some of us this is a tall order, and first we need to face some of our deepest fears. Fear itself sometimes drives people to seek out survival skills—that apocalypse-survival crowd of preppers, zombie killers, conspiracy theorists, and the like. *Survivalists* are surely part of the survival skills movement. But the motivation for those folks is radically different than what we've been exploring here. Besides, in my experience folks who have those kinds of motivations often change dramatically once they connect with their own primal nature.

More important, I believe being connected to a community of people who actively practice invaluable skills like those described in this book and who have developed trust and excellent communication is what we are all really looking for.

The reality is that, for most of human history, that's exactly the kind of community we all lived in: one based on deep knowledge of and connection to place, practical skills to survive and thrive in that place, and layers of community and trust based on a lifetime of shared experience. When people express interest in the primal movement and come to a survival skills class or end up enrolling in a survival immersion program they are, ultimately, searching for a place to belong—in other words, a longing for the intact, connected village.

Many years ago, while at Malalo, I was deep in conversation with fellow WAS instructors trying to solve the tricky challenge of wrapping up the end of the year for the Anake program while also wrapping up teen and kid programs at the same time. This would be the first time we would have all the programs together at the end of the year, and we discussed the role of rites of passage in our final ceremony.

Rites of passage are a big topic in the survival skills movement and a sophisticated field of study, but the boiled-down version is that, at important junctures in life, we long for, and even need, an ordeal and ceremony of some kind that marks important changes for ourselves. Such ordeals need to be witnessed and recognized by others besides ourselves—ideally, our friends, family, and community. While we have some examples of rites of passage such as confirmations, bar mitzvahs, and quinceaneras, deeper challenges that also focus on our abilities to survive and thrive in the natural world are a longing that lingers for many.

In our conversation, we crafted an idea to merge all of the programs together to witness a final, overnight rite of passage experience for our teens. The teens would go out and create a solo fire using a bow-drill or hand-drill to get their fire. Adult students would be supporters, staff would hold the center, and the younger kids would get to witness the going out and coming back, knowing that someday they might get to do the same thing. That conversation ended up leading to the first-ever rite of passage named FireQuest, and it was epic, wild, and a little rocky, but, boy, did it change a lot of people involved. I still have conversations with some of the teens involved in that event over 15 years ago.

How do you wrap up the year for people who've been immersed in their own experience of deep nature connection, learning survival skills, and interacting with their own little community? How do you prepare them to enter back into the rest of the world with its 9–5 work schedule, social media, grocery stores, Amazon, and all the other aspects of modernity that they had left behind, at least for a little while?

The answer brings us full circle back to Malalo, and the students we met in Chapter 1 who had such a hard survival immersion trip and had their asses kicked by the wet, rain, and cold, but who emerged stronger, more resilient, and more vibrant. After all they'd endured and experienced, how do you prepare them for their return to society? These were students who had made fire by hand, built and stayed in survival shelters for multiple nights, had tracked wild animals, butchered their own meat, and had started to learn in great depth every plant, bird, mammal, insect, and tree in the surrounding bioregion. What could we do for them?

The answer? Have them become part of a village, even if for just a day or two, and to help shepherd an overnight fire experience for the younger generations. Let them have a taste of that regenerative, intact, ecological village.

Not everyone likes FireQuest. But, I can honestly say that most people love it. It becomes a shield against the re-entry into a world that doesn't understand what has happened to you. Fire-Quest is filled with so many layers of people and culture wrapped together to watch a group of preteens or teens go out in some ancient way to tend a fire all night by themselves. There is just enough edge and danger for the students to struggle, triumph, and grow with the support of the adults—the protectors, facilitators, and supporters—around them.

FireQuest culminates the morning after the students are done with their fire. Quite a bit after dawn, they are walked back through the forest silently after they have put out their fires and gently returned their fire site to the land. Students are held some distant from Malalo, and then, at the appropriate signal, they are sung back into the hut. Inside the hut, they are placed on stumps of honor near the fire and surrounded by layers of adults, elders, parents, and community to hear their stories—their struggles, triumphs, challenges, and, of course, how they have changed.

Hearing them hesitantly share their stories of what it was like to spend a whole night by themselves, tending a fire, stirs everyone in attendance. But for the adult students of the program, who only a week before were coming back from their own survival trip, deep emotional resonance is created with the youth before them. Some are so stirred by the experience that they vow to take this up as their own work. Many go on to start their own survival schools and lead their own version of this awakening and enlivening process.

What do people do after they've had a deep discovery of their primal nature and their longing for deep connection and community like the ones described above?

On the extremes, people revert back to the life they had before or they are inspired to start their own programs for others to experience their own primal nature. The majority simply integrate these teachings and skills into their lives with their friends and families—and there are more and more people walking around with these kinds of experiences as part of their life, seeking to build a new way forward with our primal nature integrated into a world that works for all.

How do we start to take this journey ourselves? What if we don't have the time, money, and opportunity to go live in the wilds for a year deeply pursuing these things?

Look at this book as a blueprint, maybe even a roadmap. Start simple. Walk into the woods. Spend time in nature. Allow your bare feet to touch the warm earth every now and again. Practice making fire. Learn to make things by hand more, and gather some wild berries or greens. Take time to learn about and connect to the animals, plants, trees, and creatures in your local area. Start listening to the birds. Play with your children outside, and let them play outside as much as they want to and as much as you can get them to. And, perhaps most importantly, find like-minded people: your village. Find ways to go on epic adventures together. Gather together once a month regularly. Have a potluck with wild foods. Build and sit around a fire together and let the kids play barefoot. Tell stories around the fire, and sing and dance as you feel called. And remember your ancient self. Remember what it means to be human. And let this inform your life as you go forward, one step at a time.

Afterword

The Ancient Lifeways Institute is no more.

John Five Bears White passed away in 2006. During the writing of this book, I talked with survival skills and deep nature connection specialists from all over the country. As has pretty much always been the case, nobody had ever heard of the Ancient Lifeways Institute—the place where my own primal journey began. John's work with ALI was profound and powerful, but it was also small scale and very much ahead of its time.

This void of people knowing John or ALI changed during my interview with Tamarack Song. It turns out that Tamarack not only knew John but had collaborated with him back in the 80s and early 90s, as they worked on similar visions.

While the school that John started is no more and his family has moved on to pursue other passions and endeavors, I wonder what it would be like for John to see the world now. The vision, ideas, and basis that formed the core of his work and what he was trying to do now are all over the place. Ancient lifeways are a core part of what is taught at survival skills school across the world. They are a part of the Stone Age living skills gatherings, a key element of survival skills–themed television shows, and a key to running successful deep nature connection programs for kids that are now sprouting up all over the place.

While the Ancient Lifeways Institute may be no more, ancient lifeways are sprouting up everywhere—his vision and legacy lives on, probably in ways he never suspected.

Acknowledgments

A book like this doesn't come out of nowhere, and there are numerous people to thank and appreciate for helping make it happen.

First of all I want to thank the White family, including Jonah, Watie, Mark, Carly, and, of course, John and Ela, may they rest in peace.

Thanks to my wife, Karen Joy Fletcher, for all her loving kindness and support.

Special thanks to Ted Alvarez for really prodding me and inspiring me to write this book after our conversations and connections over many years.

Also, special thanks to Katie Benoit, my editor at Falcon, for being such an incredibly easy and gifted person to work with and for taking a chance on something new and outside the box.

I want to thank all the people who agreed to be interviewed for this book. Not all the interviews made it, but I appreciate it nonetheless. Thanks for sharing your primal stories with me!

Another big round of special thanks to Jon Young and Harrison Moretz for being such amazing mentors, teachers, and role models in my life for many years.

Big shouts out to all of the Wilderness Awareness School staff past, present, and future. Thanks for the amazing, impactful, important work you do! Also, special thanks to the AOS, ALP, and Community School grads from all of the years.

Acknowledgments

Extended thanks to the worldwide primal community, including the 8 Shields schools, survival schools and teachers, the ancient living skills scene, the deep nature connection folks, and others doing this kind of work.

Thanks in loving memory to Ingwe, Gilbert Walking Bull, Chris Kenworthy, and Jake Swamp.

And extended love to my family, including my daughters, Katie and Tara, my son, Orion, and my parents and extended family. Thanks for supporting my primal path!

Finally, thanks to the readers of this book, followers of my blog, and students I've gotten to coach, mentor, and work with over the years!

190

Primal's Cast of Characters

Alexia Allen

Alexia and I were instructors at the Anake Program together while we were staff at Wilderness Awareness School. Alexia is a superb naturalist, bird language expert, and the founder of Hawthorn Farm. She and her partner Daniel Kirchhof have undertaken numerous food and survival challenges, including spending a whole year eating only what they had grown, gathered, raised, hunted, and foraged.

www.hawthornfarm.org

Nicole Apelian

Nicole Apelian, PhD, is a scientist, mother, educator, researcher, expeditionary leader, safari guide, herbalist, and traditional skills instructor. Nicole has been a star on the show *Alone*, demonstrating her survival and primal skills by lasting 57 days alone in the wilds of British Columbia. She also has worked extensively with the Kalahari Bushmen including co-leading trips with Jon Young.

www.nicoleapelian.com

Steven Barnes

Steven is a self-described Afro-futurist as well as being a prolific author and screenwriter. His books explore the deep theme of our underlying primal nature and instincts as well as serving as an exploration of the impact of the African diaspora on our collective mythological consciousness. Steven has studied and taught martial arts for a number of years, as well as developed many personal growth training programs. His books include *Great Sky Woman, Iron Shadows, Lion's Blood,* and most recently *Twelve Days.*

www.stevenbarneslife.wordpress.com

Tom Brown Jr.

Raised by an Apache elder and mentor named Stalking Wolf, Tom Brown Jr. is the founder of the Tracker School based in New Jersey. Tom is the author of more than a dozen books including the worldwide bestseller *The Tracker* and is one of the primary people responsible for the explosive growth of the survival skills and primal movement worldwide. Tom has especially brought the fields of tracking and awareness to the greater field of survival skills emphasized and taught around the world.

www.trackerschool.com

Tony Deis

Tony Deis has started one of the most successful deep nature connection and survival skills schools in the world: Trackers Earth. Tony's programs reach thousands of youth and adults in Portland and the Bay Area.

www.trackersearth.com

Mick Dodge

Mick grew up wild and free running through the wild lands of what he calls OM (the Olympic Mountains). Growing up with his dad in Japan and spending time with uncles and grandfathers on the Olympic Peninsula, Mick developed his own deep nature connection practices and philosophy. Mick was the star of the National Geographic show *The Legend of Mick Dodge.* He is a strong advocate of time spent barefoot and in nature immersion and teaches his own form of natural movement and strength training known as Earthgym.

Tom Elpel

Founder and creator of OWLS, LLC and Green University, LLC, Tom has been active in the Stone Age living skills movement for decades. He has written numerous books including *Botany in a Day* and *Foraging the Mountain West*. Tom was one of the first instructors at Rabbitstick Rendezvous.

www.hollowtop.com

Ingwe

Born Norman Powell and later given the name Ingwe in honor of his experiences with leopards, Ingwe co-founded Wilderness Awareness School and served as its first elder and grandfather. Ingwe passed away in 2005. His ashes were scattered around the building Malalo ya Chui, an Akamba-style hut based on the main property of Wilderness Awareness School and the place of its central fire.

Sheina Lew-Levy

Originally from Quebec, Sheina is a graduate of the Anake Program at Wilderness Awareness School. She has gone on to travel the world and study with people such as the Cree community in northern Canada, indigenous hunter-gatherers in the Congo, and to study tracking in South Africa. Sheina recently completed her PhD from the University of Cambridge with a focus on hunter-gatherer childhoods.

Larry Dean Olsen

Larry Dean Olsen is one of the other chief founders and creators of the modern survival skills movement. He created programs at BYU that eventually grew into the Boulder Outdoor Survival

School (one of the best known schools in the world), wrote the classic survival skills book *Outdoor Survival Skills,* and co-started Rabbitstick Rendezvous—the first of many Stone Age living skills gatherings. He passed away in late 2018.

Dave Scott

Dave Scott is a tracker, naturalist, and survival skills instructor who is the founder of Earth Native school outside of Austin, Texas. Dave has successfully reached thousands of youth and adults through his programs, growing a hugely successful school in under a decade. He is the co-author of *Bird Feathers: A Guide to North American Species.*

Tamarack Song

Founder of Teaching Drum Outdoor School, Tamarack is an elder in the field of survival and Stone Age living skills. Tamarack has his own survival immersion program as well as a community of people based around living a primal life. He is the author of *Entering the Mind of the Trackers* and *Journey to the Ancestral Self.*

www.tamaracksong.com
www.teachingdrum.com

Gene Tagaban

Gene is a teacher, dancer, performer, storyteller, healer, and mentor of Native Alaskan, Filipino, and Cherokee descent. He has been a teacher and mentor at the Wilderness Awareness School as a guest instructor at the Anake Program and at the Art of Mentoring. Gene has brought deep nature connection and survival skills practices back to children and adults in Native communities.

Tony Ten Fingers

Tony is a Lakota teacher and mentor who served as an honorary "uncle" to many of the early Wilderness Awareness School staff. He has taught and shared in wilderness therapy settings as well as on reservations where he has done work with suicide prevention, job training, and mentoring for Native youth and adults. Tony has also served as faculty at different Native colleges and is the author of *Lakota Wisdom.*

Lynx Vilden
Lynx is well known in the larger Stone Age living skills and survival skills movement for being one of the premier female instructors in the world, and for her numerous forays into the wilderness with students for weeks and even months at a time, living fully in the Stone Age for extended periods of time.

www.lynxvilden.com

John White
A Native teacher of Shawnee and Cherokee descent, White founded the Ancient Lifeways Institute and taught many traditional skills including flintknapping, pottery making, cordage, and the building of traditional houses. Perhaps most importantly he was the carrier of a vast oral tradition lineage. He was my first teacher and mentor in Stone Age living skills. John passed away in 2006.

Jonah White
Son of John White and one of the chief instructors at the Ancient Lifeways Institute (ALI), Jonah was my first tracking and deep nature connection mentor along with his brother Watie. Jonah read a lot of Tom Brown Jr.'s books growing up which influenced his path of deep nature connection, tracking, and hunting. Jonah has gone on to become a wildly successful entrepreneur and businessman, founding his own company, Billy Bob Products, Inc. He maintains a hunting lodge and a large number of rehabilitated wild animals at his home near the previous location of ALI.

www.billybobproducts.com

Watie White

Son of John and another instructor at ALI, Watie was another key mentor, teacher, and role model in my life around primal skills. Watie is now a very successful artist based in Omaha, Nebraska.

www.watiewhite.com

Jon Young

Tom Brown's first student and one of the main inheritors of his teachings around survival, awareness, and tracking, Jon has gone on to teach around the world founding organizations such as Wilderness Awareness School and 8Shields.org. Jon has studied with numerous other teachers including Gilbert Walking Bull, Jake Swamp, and more recently San Bushmen elders in the Kalahari. Jon is the author of *What the Robin Knows* and coined the term and concepts of bird language. Jon Young also started the Art of Mentoring, which has had a huge impact on the homeschooling and free-range kids movement.

www.8shields.org

Index

About the Author

Nate Summers, M.Ac., has been a survival skills instructor for more than twenty years with a background in anthropology, Asian studies, and natural medicine. He taught and directed at the Wilderness Awareness School for over fifteen years where he helped to start both the Anake Outdoor School and the Anake Leadership Program. Nate's passions include ethnobotany, natural mentoring, hunter-gatherer childhoods, natural movement, herbal medicine, internal martial arts, and leadership. He helped found the Vashon Wilderness Program and Outdoor Connections, and has served as a naturalist for King County Parks and Seattle Parks and Rec.

Nate holds a master's degree from NIAOM (Northwest Institute of Acupuncture and Oriental Medicine) and B.A.s in both anthropology and Asian studies from the University of Illinois. He has served as faculty for the Desert Institute of Healing Arts, the Asian Institute of Medical Studies, and as adjunct faculty for Prescott College. Nate likes to fish, practice internal martial arts, go on adventures with his family, and gather wild foods and medicine.